Library Instruction

Library Instruction
A *Bibliography, 1975 Through 1985*

compiled by
Tian-Chu Shih

McFarland & Company, Inc., Publishers
Jefferson, North Carolina, and London

Library of Congress Cataloguing-in-Publication Data

Shih, Tian-Chu, 1958–
   Library instruction, a bibliography, 1975 through 1985.

   Includes index.
   1. Library orientation — Bibliography. 2. Bibliography
   — Methodology — Study and teaching — Bibliography.
   I. Title.
   Z711.2.S533   1986   016.0255'6   86-42607

ISBN 0-89950-236-9 (sewn softcover; acid-free natural paper) ∞

Printed in the United States of America

McFarland & Company, Inc., Publishers,
   Box 611, Jefferson, North Carolina 28640

To My Husband Tim

Contents

Preface

It is the duty of an instructional librarian to help people obtain optimal use of the library. How to achieve new ideals and improve on library instruction is my major on-the-job concern. Currently, this field has no single-volume bibliographies in print. This book is designed to enable librarians to more easily gather information on library instruction.

In preparing this work which is up-to-date through December 31, 1985, standard relevant reference works and trade lists were consulted. The bibliography is in four sections: Libraries in General, Academic Libraries, School Libraries, and Public Libraries. A different letter is used for every section and works within each are numbered. This numbering system is especially helpful in the Title Keyword Index. Under each keyword, the user can immediately separate articles about academic libraries from other libraries. An Author Index is also included.

I thank my husband, Tim, for his generous support.

Tian-Chu Shih
Spring 1986

Libraries in General

G001. Adams, R. J. "Teaching Packages for Library User Education." <u>Audiovisual Librarian</u> 3 (Winter 1976-77): 100-6.

G002. Allen, M. "TV Technique Is Fighting TV." <u>Library Association Record</u> 78 (September 1976): 427.

G003. Anstine, F. A. "Library Instruction and Disabled Individuals." <u>Illinois Libraries</u> 63 (September 1981): 535-9.

G004. Bailey, E. C. "Comparative Reviews: library guides and handbooks." <u>Reference Services Review</u> 11 (Spring 1983): 47-53.

G005. Batt, F. "Education Is Illogical!" <u>Improving College and University Teaching</u> 25 (Summer 1977): 188.

G006. Beckman, M. and Langmead, S. "Library Signage." <u>Show-Me Libraries</u> 31 (June 1980): 5-8.

G007. Blazek, Ron. <u>Influencing Students Toward Media Center Use: an experimental investigation in mathematics.</u> Chicago: American Library Association, 1975.

G008. Breivik, Patricia Senn. <u>Planning the Library Instruction Program.</u> Chicago: American Library Association, 1982.

G009. Brundin, Robert E. "Education for Instructional Librarians; development and overview." <u>Journal of Education for Library and Information Science</u> 25 (Winter 1985): 177-89.

G010. Cameron, D. B. "Independence and the Library." <u>Library Journal</u> 109 (January 1984): 51.

G011. Carmichael, J. V. "Hands-Off Instruction: a study of the effectiveness of a media-based library instruction module." <u>Georgia Librarian</u> 18 (November 1981): 4-6.

G012. Chandler, G. How to Find Out; Printed and On-Line Sources. 5th ed. New York: Pergamon, 1982.

G013. Chapman, L. "User Education Game." New Library World 82 (October 1981): 186-8.

G014. Chiang, K. S. and Kautz, B. "The Malti's Chicken: a different kind of video." Research Strategies 3 (Summer 1985): 143-6.

G015. Chittenden, C. B. "New Signs in Old Buildings." Research Strategies 2 (Winter 1984): 45-6

G016. Clark, D. "Helping Librarians to Help Their Users." Unesco Bulletin for Libraries 32 (November 1978): 35-7.

G017. Cook, M. G. New Library Key. 3rd ed. New York: Wilson, 1975.

G018. Culkin, P. B. and Walker, E. "Computers in User Education." Reference Services Review 12 (Winter 1984): 75-8.

G019. Currie, M. and Others. "Evaluating the Relationship Between Library Skills and Library Instruction." Canadian Library Journal 39 (February 1982): 35-7.

G020. Czisny, J. "Evaluating Skills Programs; Definitions and Steps." Wisconsin Library Bulletin 75 (March 1979): 59-61.

G021. Dittman, M. "Standards for Library Skills? A Viewpoint." Wisconsin Library Bulletin 76 (March/April 1980): 70.

G022. Doelker, Richard E. and Toifel, Peggy. "The Development of a Self-Guided, Library-Based Materials and Methods Manual for Social Work Research." Behavioral & Social Sciences Librarian 3 (Summer 1984): 81-93.

G023. Douthwaite, M. "Learning Resource Center Orientation On Tape." Previews 4 (May 1976): 9.

G024. Elkins, Elizabeth A., et al. Developing Printed Materials for Library Instruction. Annual New York Library Association Meeting, Lake Placid, N.Y., October 16, 1976. New York: New York Library Instruction Clearinghouse, 1976.

G025. Ellsbury, Susan H. and Rafferty, Randy. Reach Out and Teach: library instruction in Mississippi libraries. Script for Slide Presentation. Mississippi: Mississippi State University, University Libraries, 1984. (ERIC Document Reproduction Service No. ED 245699).

G026. Essary, K. and Parker, S. "Educating Your Patrons." Arkansas Libraries 32 (1975): 26-9.

G027. Fabian, W. M. "CALICO: skills programs to promote library use." American Libraries 15 (April 1984): 264.

G028. Farber, Evan Ira, and Kirk, Thomas G. "Instruction in Library Use." ALA Yearbook (1976): 59.

G029. Farley, L. "User Education." Texas Library Journal 61 (Summer 1985): 40-1.

G030. Fitzgerald, S. "Effective Approach to Library Instruction in Departmental Training Courses." State Librarian 25 (July 1977): 25.

G031. Fjallbrant, Nancy. "Evaluation in a User Education Programme." Journal of Librarianship 9 (April 1977): 83-95.

G032. Fjallbrant, Nancy and Sjostrand, B. "Bridging the Gap: library user education to new user categories." Tidskrift for Dokumentation 39 (1983): 106-10.

G033. Fox, Peter. "Library Handbooks: an international viewpoint." Libri 27 (December 1977): 296-304.

G034. Freedman, Janet L. and Bantly, Harold A. comps. Information Searching; A Handbook for Designing & Creating Instructional Programs. rev. ed. California: Coaroorow, 1902.

G035. Frick, Elizabeth. "Humanizing Technology Through Instruction." Canadian Library Journal 41 (October 1984): 263-7.

G036. Fudge, L. L. Individualized Instruction In Using the Readers' Guide Applying Aptitude Treatment Interaction. California: University of Southern California, 1979.

G037. Gawith, G. "Information Technology and Educational

Librarianship." New Zealand Libraries 44 (March 1985): 157-9.

G038. Gebhard, Patricia. "How to Evaluate Library Instructional Programs." California Librarian 37 (April 1976): 36-43.

G039. George, Mary W. and Hogan, Sharon A. "What's 3 x 5 and full of holes?" Research Strategies (Winter 1984): 50-5.

G040. "Georgia State University Workshop, Planning for Effective Library Instruction." Georgia Librarian 15 (November 1978): 46.

G041. Gilliam, B. H. "Beyond Bibliographic Instruction [workshop for the secretaries and key clerical personnel on campus]." Southeastern Librarian 31 (Spring 1981): 8-10.

G042. Gorden, Charlotte. How to Find What You Want in the Library. Woodbury, New York: Barron's Educational Series, 1978.

G043. Gunjal, S. R. and Asundi, A. Y. "User Education and Training." Herald of Library Science 23 (January-April 1984): 16-23.

G044. Hanson, J. R. "Evaluation of Library User Education With Reference to the Programme at Dorset Institute of Higher Education (DIHE)." Journal of Librarianship 16 (January 1984): 1-18.

G045. Hardendorff, J. B. Libraries and How to Use Them. New York: Watts, 1979.

G046. Harding, G. "Workshop Reports: Teaching Library Concepts." Pacific Northwest Library Association Quarterly 48 (Fall 1983): 26-7.

G047. Harris, C. "Illuminative Evaluation of User Education Programmes." Aslib Proceedings 29 (October 1977): 348-62.

G048. Harris, K. G. E. "User Education." Libri 32 (December 1982): 327-36.

G049. Hartley, A. A. "Hey That's Love Story!" North Carolina Libraries 34 (Spring 1976): 23-4.

G050. Hartmann, J. S. and Hartmann, R. R. "Inviting Design Helps the User: Any Library Can Have Pleasing Colors and Signs." Wisconsin Library Bulletin 73 (July 1977): 161-2.

G051. Haynes, E. "Computer Assisted Library Instruction: an annotated bibliography." Colorado Libraries 11 (March 1985): 31-5.

G052. Hillard, James M. Where to Find What: a handbook to reference service. Metuchen, NJ.: Scarecrow, 1984.

G053. Hills, P. J. and Others. Evaluation of Tape-Slide Guides for Library Instruction. England: British Lib., 1978.

G054. Hodges, G. G. "Library-Use Instruction: the librarian's challenge and responsibility." Catholic Library World 53 (November 1981): 176-9.

G055. Hoplinson, Shirley L. ed. Instructional Materials for Teaching the Use of the Library. 5th ed. San Jose, Calfornia: Claremont House, 1975.

G056. Horton, W. J. "Painless, Professional Library Tour; Day or Night." Unabashed Librarian 23 (1977): 10.

G057. Huston, M, M. and Parson, W. L. " A Model of Librarianship for Combining Learning and Teaching." Research Strategies 3 (Spring 1985): 75-80.

G058. Irving, A. "Educating Users — Is There Really a New Approach?" RQ 20 (Fall 1980): 11-4.

G059. Jaramillo, G. R. ed. "Status of Library Instruction in Colorado Libraries." Colorado Libraries 9 (June 1983): 4-28.

G060. Jay, H. L. Stimulating Student Search: library media/classroom teacher techniques. Hamden, Conn.: Library Professional, 1983.

G061. Jonassen, David H. Nonbook Media: a self-paced instructional handbook for teachers and library media personnel. Hamden, Conn.: Library Professional Publications, 1982.

G062. Kenney, D. J. "Universal Library Skills: an outdated concept." Southeastern Librarian 30 (Spring 1980): 13-4.

G063. Kirk, Thomas. "Past, Present, and Future of Library Instruction." Southeastern Librarian 27 (Spring 1977): 15-8.

G064. Kosterman, W. "Guide to Library Environmental Graphics." Library Technology Reports 14 (May 1978): 269-95.

G065. Kouns, B. "Guiding Students Through the Reader's Guide." California Media and Library Educators Association Journal 1 (Fall 1977): 26-7.

G066. Kupersmith, J. J. "Design Model for Instructional Graphics." Research Strategies 2 (Summer 1984): 136-8.

G067. Laburn, C. "User Guidance and Training." South African Journal of Library and Information Science 52 (August 1984): 93-8.

G068. Lasher, E. and Hibbs, J. "Creating a Slide Tape Library Orientation Program." Ohio Media Spectrum 30 (January 1978): 76-7.

G069. Leeper, D. P. and Hall, J. B. eds. "Mediated Approaches to Library Instruction." Drexel Library Quarterly (January 1980).

G070. Lester, R. "Why Educate the Library User?" Aslib Proceedings 31 (August 1979): 366-80.

G071. Library Association. Working Party on Training. Training in Libraries: report of the Library Association Working Party on Training. London: Library Association. Working Party on Training, 1977.

G072. "Library Instruction." Catholic Library World 49 (February 1978): 275-81.

G073. "Library Instruction: linkage to the future." Arkansas Libraries 42 (June 1985): 4-26.

G074. Library Instruction Programs 1975: a Wisconsin directory. Madison: Wisconsin Library Association, 1975.

G075. "Library Orientation and User Instruction." Alabama Librarian 26 (September 1975): 8+.

G076. Lilly, M. "Collecting User Education Materials in

Australia: the role of USER." <u>IATUL Proceedings</u> 15 (1983): 81-8.

G077. Lindsay, M. "Catching the Eye: Library Signs of Oslo." <u>Library Association Record</u> 82 (July 1980): 319.

G078. Livingston, B. "N. Y. Graphics Seminar: signs for better access." <u>Library Journal</u> 104 (February 1979): 343-4.

G079. Lockwood, D. L. comp. <u>Library Instruction: a bibliography.</u> Connecticut: Greenwood, 1979.

G080. Lolley, J. L. and Watkins, R. "Use of Audio-Visuals in Developing Favorable Attitudes Toward Library Instruction." <u>Educational Technology</u> 19 (September 1979): 56-8.

G081. Lubans, John. "Mediated Instruction: an overview with emphasis on evaluation." <u>Drexel Library Quarterly</u> 16 (January 1980): 27-40.

G082. Lubans, John, ed. <u>Progress in Educating the Library User.</u> New York: Bowker, 1978.

G083. Lynch, Mary Jo. "Tour to Tour: a new approach to the guided tour." <u>Research Quarterly</u> 11 (Fall 1976): 46-8.

G084. Mallery, M. S. and DeVore, R. E. <u>Sign Systems for Libraries.</u> Chicago: American Library Association, 1982.

G085. Malley, Ian. <u>The Basics of Information Skills Teaching.</u> London, Eng.: Clive Bingley, 1984.

G086. Malley, Ian, ed. <u>Educating the User.</u> Papers given at a two-day course held at the Library Association on 16 and 17 November, 1977. London, Eng.: Library Association, 1979.

G087. Marshall, P. "Our Role As Rescue-Educators in an Age of Basic Needs Information." <u>Library Association Record</u> 84 (February 1982): 57-8.

G088. Martinelli, J. "Bilingual Slide-Tape Library Orientation." <u>Audiovisual Instruction</u> 21 (January 1976): 55-6.

G089. McClure, Charles R. <u>Chickasha Cooperative</u>

Bibliographic Instruction Project: final evaluation.
ERIC Document Reproduction Service, 1981. (ERIC
Document Reproduction Service No. ED 203860).

G090. McElroy, A. R. and Bate, J. L. "User Education --
For Life?" Library Review 31 (Spring 1982): 3-10.

G091. McGowan, O. T. P. "Library Instruction Needed."
Catholic Library World 48 (November 1976): 185.

G092. Mead, G. "Long Goodbye [importance of user
education]." New Library World 80 (August 1979): 146-
7.

G093. Mealy, Virginia. Library Skills: activities and
games. Minneapolis: Denison, 1981.

G094. Morris, Jacquelyn and Webster, Donald F.
Developing Objectives for Library Instruction. Annual
New York Library Association Meeting, Lake Placid,
N.Y. October 16, 1976. New York: New York Library
Instruction Clearinghouse, 1976.

G095. Morton, B. "For the Record: a library instruction
profile form." Minnesota Libraries 25 (Summer 1978):
311-4.

G096. M'Queen, I. "AVSCOT Viewing Session, Glasgow,
Wednesday, 29 February 1984." [user education
programmes from around the UK]. Audiovisual
Librarian 10 (Summer 1984): 151-2.

G097. Nahl-Jakobovits, Diane and Jakobovits, Leon A.
"Managing the Effective Micro-Information
Environment." Research Strategies 3 (Winter 1985):
17-28.

G098. North Carolina. Department of Public Instruction.
Division of Educational Media. "Educational Media
Competency Goals and Performance Indicators." North
Carolina Libraries 38 (Fall 1980): 17-27.

G099. Norton, M. and Baine, B. "All the Best People
"Calendar Clue."" Louisiana Library Association
Bulletin 41 (Spring 1979): 87-8.

G100. O'Brien, R. and Soderman, J. eds. Basic Guide to
Research Sources. New York: New American Library,
1975.

G101. O'Connor, J. E. "Index-In-Dice, How to Use Periodical Indexes and Abstracting Services." Audiovisual Instruction 21 (November 1976): 40-2.

G102. Orna, E. "Should We Educate Our Users?" Aslib Proceedings 30 (April 1978): 130-41.

G103. Patterson, T. H. "Library Skills Workshops for Support Personnel." RQ 19 (Summer 1980): 351-3.

G104. Payne, J. H. "Plan Is the Design -- Preparation for an Audiovisual Script." Colorado Libraries 9 (June 1983): 37-42.

G105. Pearce, R. "Functions of Visuals in Tape-Slide Instructional Programmes." Audiovisual Librarian 10 (Winter 1984): 18-23.

G106. Phipps, S. "Why Use Workbooks? Or, Why Do The Chickens Cross the Road? And Other Metaphors, Mixed." Drexel Library Quarterly 16 (January 1980): 41-53.

G107. Plotnik, A. "Bibliolaffic Instruction." American Libraries 16 (September 1985): 533.

G108. Pollet, Dorothy. "New Directions in Library Signage: you can get there from here." Wilson Library Bulletin 50 (February 1979): 456-62.

G109. Pollet, Dorothy. "Signs Are For People." South Carolina Librarian 23 (Fall 1979): 2-7.

G110. Pollet, Dorothy, and Haskell, Peter. Sign Symbols for Libraries: solving the way finding problem. New York: Bowker, 1979.

G111. Rader, Hannelore B. "Library Orientation and Instruction, 1979." Reference Services Review 8 (January 1980): 31-46.

G112. Rader, Hannelore B. "Library Orientation and Instruction -- 1980." Reference Services Review 9 (April 1981): 79-89.

G113. Rader, Hannelore B. "Library Orientation and Instruction -- 1981." Reference Services Review 10 (Summer 1982): 33-41.

G114. Rader, Hannelore B. "Library Orientation and Instruction -- 1982." Reference Services Review 11 (Summer 1983): 57-65.

G115. Rader, Hannelore B. "Mediated Library Instruction: an annotated bibliography." Drexel Library Quarterly 16 (January 1980): 116-33.

G116. Reynolds, C. J. "Discovering the Government Documents Collection in Libraries." RQ 14 (Spring 1975): 228-31.

G117. Reynolds, L. And Barett, S. Signs and Guiding for Libraries. London: Bingley, 1981.

G118. Richards, M. "National Library User Education Programme for Teachers." Singapore Libraries 14 (1984): 27-30.

G119. Ridgeway, P. M. "Coordination of Bibliographic Instruction Programs/Instruction Round-Up." South Carolina Librarian 25 (Spring 1981): 9-10.

G120. Rosenblum, J. "Future of Reference Service: death by complexity?" Wilson Library Bulletin 52 (December 1977): 300-1.

G121. Rosenblum, J. "Towards an Alternative to the In-House Tour." Southeastern Librarian 28 (Winter 1978): 235-8.

G122. Ruckl, S. and Hulpusch, G. "Present Level and Organisation of the User Training in the German Democratic Republic." International Forum on Information and Documentation 7 (April 1982): 31-5.

G123. Rushton, Doris. How to Use a Library. London: Peter Daffon Association, 1980.

G124. Schmidt, J. "Reader Education in the Eighties." Australian Library Journal 30 (August 1981): 97-104.

G125. Segal, J. D. and McNally, T. "Battle of the Library Superstars; the Use of Professional Media Production Techniques." Library Journal 108 (April 1983): 795-7.

G126. Shanklin, S. I. Behavioral Evaluation of Library Skills Instruction. Mo: University of Missouri, 1981.

G127. Simon, R. comp. "Library Use Instruction: curricular support or curricular integration?" North Carolina Libraries 38 (Fall 1980): 4-37.

G128. Smith, B. G. "Videotape the Only Way." Library Association Record 78 (April 1976): 177.

G129. "The Source: Instruction." American Libraries 14 (December 1983). 750; 15 (April 1984): 266; 15 (June 1984): 464-5; 15 (September 1984): 607; 15 (November 1984): 747-8.

G130. Stamps, D. C. "Out of the Woodwork: orienting the 'invisible' faculty." Georgia Librarian 21 (November 1984): 90-2.

G131. Stoffle, Carla J. and Others, Comps. Library Instruction Programs, 1975: a Wisconsin directory. Wisconsin: Wisconsin Library Association, 1975.

G132. Stoffle, Carla J. and Pryor, J. M. "Competency-Based Education and Library Instruction." Library Trends 29 (Summer 1980): 55-67.

G133. Strawn, R. R. Topics, Terms, and Research Techniques: self-instruction in using library catalogs. California: Scarecrow, 1980.

G134. Streatfield, D. R. and Others. "Problem-Based Training Approach to Information for Practitioners." Libri 31 (September 1981): 243-57.

G135. Svnicki, M. D. "Getting Down to the Basics of Teaching." Catholic Library World 56 (March 1985): 335-7.

G136. Swanson, R. "Signage in Hard-Edge: new sign design concepts." Nebraska Library Association Quarterly 10 (Spring 1979): 2-7.

G137. Taylor, P. J. "User Education and the Role of Evaluation." Unesco Bulletin for Libraries 32 (July 1978): 252-9.

G138. Taylor, Peter J. and Others. Education of Users of Library and Information Services: an international bibliography. 1926-1976. London: Aslib, 1979.

G139. Tessmer, M. "Reference Poster." Unabashed Librarian 46 (1983): 30.

G140. Thompson, A. H. "Scriptwriting for Audiovisual Presentations." Audiovisual Librarian 7 (Autumn 1981): 23-8.

G141. Tippet, H. "Word Processing and Records Management Applications." Reference Services Review 12 (Winter 1984): 73-5.

G142. Tuckett, H. W. and Stoffle, Carla J. "Learning
       Theory and the Self-Reliant Library User." RQ 24
       (Fall 1984): 58-66.

G143. Webb, C. Anne. "Modeling Recreational Reading: a
       model." English Journal 74 (September 1985): 82-3.

G144. Welch, C. B. "User Education." Texas Library Journal
       60 (Spring 1984): 22-3.

G145. "Why BI or LI." Reference Services Review 12 (Spring
       1984): 59-66.

G146. Wood, V. "New Jersey Clearinghouse for Library User
       Education." New Jersey Libraries 12 (April 1979): 13-
       14.

Academic Libraries

A001. "Academic Library Outreach Program: University of California, Irvine." Library Journal 108 (March 15, 1983): 540-1.

A002. Adams, M. "Bibliographic Instruction in Academic Libraries." Catholic Library World 52 (April 1981): 397-9.

A003. Ahmad, C. F. "8th Annual LOEX [Library orientation/instruction exchange] Conference." Oklahoma Librarian 28 (October 1978): 18+.

A004. Akinyode, S. A. "User Education in a Nigerian University Library: its problems and prospects in Ibadan University library." Nigerian Library and Information Science Review 2 (May-November 1984): 109-24).

A005. Alfors, Inez Larson and Loe, Mary Hong. "Foremothers and Forefathers: one way to preserve and enhance the library research paper." Research Strategies 3 (Winter 1985): 4-16.

A006. Allen, S. N. and Others. "Implementation of a Large-Scale Self-Instructional Course in Medical Information Resources." Medical Library Association Bulletin 67 (July 1979): 302-7.

A007. Aluri, R. "Application of Learning Theories to Library-Use Instruction." Libri 31 (August 1981): 140-52.

A008. American Library Association. Association of College and Research Libraries. Bibliographic Instruction Section. "Evaluating Bibliographic Instruction: a handbook." College & Research Libraries News 8 (September 1983): 271-3.

A009. American Library Association. Association of College and Research Libraries. Bibliographic Instruction Section. "Think Tank Recommendations for Bibliographic Instruction." College & Research Libraries News No. 11 (December 1981): 394-8.

A010. American Library Association. Association of College
      and Research Libraries. Bibliographic Instruction
      Section. Continuing Education Committee. Organizing
      and Managing a Library Instruction Program:
      checklists. Chicago, Ill.: American Library
      Association, 1979.

A011. American Library Association. Association of College
      and Research Libraries. Bibliographic Instruction
      Section. Policy and Planning Committee. Bibliographic
      Instruction Handbook. Chicago: American Library
      Association, 1979.

A012. American Library Association. Association of College
      and Research Libraries. Bibliographic Instruction
      Section. Research Committee. "Dissertations in
      Bibliographic Instruction." Research Strategies 2
      (Summer 1984): 149-52; (Fall 1984): 202-7.

A013. American Library Association. Association of College
      and Research Libraries. Bibliographic Instruction
      Section. Research Committee. "Research Agenda for
      Bibliographic Instruction." College & Research
      Libraries News 4 (April 1980): 94-5.

A014. American Library Association. Association of College
      and Research Libraries. Bibliographic Instruction Task
      Force. "Draft Guidelines for Bibliographic
      Instruction in Academic Libraries." College &
      Research Libraries News No. 11 (December 1976): 301.

A015. American Library Association. Association of College
      and Research Libraries. Bibliographic Instruction Task
      Force. "Guidelines for Bibliographic Instruction in
      Academic Libraries." College & Research Libraries
      News No. 4 (April 1977): 92.

A016. American Library Association. Association of College
      and Research Libraries. Bibliographic Instruction Task
      Force. "Toward Guidelines for Bibliographic
      Instruction in Academic Libraries." College & Research
      Libraries News 5 (May 1975): 137-9.

A017. American Library Association. Association of College
      and Research Libraries. Education and Behavioral
      Sciences Section. Bibliographic Instruction for
      Educator Committee. "BI Tip Sheet for Academic
      Administrators and Support Staff; planning an
      instruction program for a neglected category of
      users." College & Research Libraries News No.10
      (November 1984): 546-8.

A018. American Library Association. Association of College
      and Research Libraries. Education and Behavioral
      Sciences Section. Bibliographic Instruction for
      Educators Committee. "Bibliographic Instruction:
      bibliographic competencies for education students."
      College & Research Libraries News no. 7 (July 1981):
      209-10.

A019. Andrews, P. "University Approach to Bibliographic
      Instruction." Bookmark 38 (Fall 1979): 219-24.

A020. Argall, Rebecca and Rudolph, Janell. Library Skills
      Handbook. Memphis, Tennessee: Metropolitan Books,
      1983.

A021. ARL Member Libraries Using Audiovisual Materials for
      Point-of-use Library Instruction. Washington:
      Association of Research Libraries, 1977.

A022. Association of Research Libraries. Systems and
      Procedures Exchange Center. User Instructions for
      Online Catalogs in ARL Libraries. Chicago:
      Association of Research Libraries. Systems and
      Procedures Exchange Center, 1983.

A023. Atkinson, R., ed. Back to the Books: bibliographic
      instruction and the theory of information sources.
      Papers presented at the 101st annual Conference of the
      American Library Association, ACRL Bibliographic
      Instruction Section, Philadelphia, 1982. Chicago:
      American Library Association, 1983.

A024. Avann, Mike and Wood, Kath eds. User Education in Art
      and Design: theory into practice. Newcastle-Upon-Tyne:
      Art Libraries Society, 1980.

A025. Bader, S. G. "A Library Skills Workshop: one
      library's experience." Medical Reference Services
      Quarterly 3 (Winter 1984): 67-70.

A026. Bailey, B. "Thesis Practicum and the Librarian's
      Role." Journal of Academic Librarianship 11 (May
      1985): 79-81.

A027. Bailey, E. R. Library Orientation-Instruction Program
      for Murray State University. Texas: George Peabody
      College for Teachers, 1977.

A028. Bailey, L. E. "Bibliographic Instruction at Hunter
      College: past, present, and future." Bookmark 38 (Fall
      1979): 257-60.

A029. Bailey, M. J. "Bibliography and Reference Aids in the Physics Library." Special Libraries 67 (April 1976): 202-7.

A030. Bain, Nancy R. and Bain, George W. "Teaching Library Resources in Geography." Journal of Geography 84 (May-June 1985): 126-8.

A031. Baker, Nancy L. Research Guide for Undergraduate Students; English and American Literature. New York: Modern Language Association of America, 1982.

A032. Baker, R. K. Doing Library Research: An Introduction for Community College Students. Boulder, Colo.: Westview Press, 1981.

A033. Baker, Robert K. Introduction to Library Research in French Literature. Boulder, Colo.: Westview, 1978.

A034. Baldwin, C. A. "Fast and Furious: a weekend session in bibliographic instruction." College & Research Libraries News 5 (May 1984): 234-5.

A035. Baldwin, J. F. and Rudolph, R. S. "Comparative Effectiveness of a Slide/Tape Show and a Library Tour." College & Research Libraries 40 (January 1979): 31-5.

A036. Baldwin, J. F. and Rudolph, R. S. "Improving Student Recall of Library Information From Slide/Tape Programs." College & Research Libraries 43 (January 1982): 78-80.

A037. Ballam, S. H. "Developing a Bibliographic Instruction Unit for the College Library." Catholic Library World 53 (November 1981): 180-1.

A038. Barr, B. G. "Information Education in the Engineering Classroom." Library Science with a Slant to Documentation 15 (June 1978): 92-8.

A039. Barry, Carol. comp. An Illinois Union List of Commercially-produced Audiovisual Materials for Bibliographic Instruction. ERIC Document Reproduction Service, 1980. (ERIC Document Reproduction Service No. ED 203881).

A040. Basic Library Skills: a self-paced introduction to the use of the Library Learning Center, University of Wisconsin-Parkside. 8th ed., rev. Kenosha: University of Wisconsin-Parkside, 1983.

A041. Beaubien, Anne K.; Hogan, Sharon A.; and George, Mary W. Learninq the Library: concepts and methods for effective bibliographic instruction. New York: Bowker, 1982.

A042. Beck, R. J. and Norris, L. "Communication Graphics in Library Orientation." Catholic Library World 17 (December 1975): 218-9.

A043. Beede, B. R. and Sadow, S. "Reference Service: from zero to total commitment." RQ 13 (Winter 1973): 147-8.

A044. Beeler, Richard J., ed. Evaluating Library Use Instruction; papers. Papers presented at the University of Denver Conference on the Evaluation of Library Use Instruction, Dec. 13-14, 1973. (Library Orientation Series: No. 4). Ann Arbor, Mich.: Pierian, 1975.

A045. Bender, C. F. Signage System for Ellis Library: an Analysis of Directional Questions. Missouri: University of Missouri, 1979.

A046. Ben-Shir, R. "Library Instruction Integrated With Patient Management." [based on a paper presented at the eighty-third annual meeting of the Medical Library Association]. Medical Library Association Bulletin 72 (July 1984): 310-1.

A047. Benson, S. "So Little for So Much." Learning Today 14 (Winter 1981): 40-6.

A048. Bergen, Kathleen and MacAdam, Barbara. "One-on-One: term paper assistance programs." RQ 24 (Spring 1985): 333-40.

A049. Bhattacharjea, S. "Orientation of Staff and Students for Better Use of the Libraries." New Frontiers in Education 8 (July-September 1978): 15-9.

A050. Bhullar, P. "LUMIN [Libraries of the University of Missouri Information Network] User Education." Show-Me Libraries 36 (August 1985): 13-18.

A051. Bhullar, P. and Timberlake, P. P. "Library Skills: an undergraduate course at the University of Missouri-Columbia." Show-Me Libraries 36 (October-November 1984): 70-4.

A052. "Bibliographic Competencies for Music Students at an Undergraduate Level." Music Library Association Notes 40 (March 1984): 529-32.

A053. "Bibliographic Instruction: a guide." Education Libraries 7 (Fall 1982): 45-60.

A054. "Bibliographic Instruction at Harvard: team named." Library Journal 103 (March 15, 1978): 604.

A055. Bibliographic Instruction Handbook. Chicago, Illinois: American Library Association, Association of College and Research Libraries, 1979. (ERIC Document Reproduction Service No. ED 188623).

A056. "Bibliographic Instruction in New England Academic Libraries." College & Research Libraries News 5 (May 1980): 152.

A057. Biggs, Mary G. and Others. Headpower! 3rd ed. ERIC Document Reproduction Service, 1977. (ERIC Document Reproduction Service No. ED 167160).

A058. Biggs, M. M. "Perils of Library Instruction." Journal of Academic Librarianship 5 (July 1979): 159.

A059. Biggs, M. M. "Preparing Tomorrow's Library User: the job that awaits us today." NYLA Bulletin 29 (June 1981): 1.

A060. BIS: what's it all about? A Manual for Committee Members of the ACRL Bibliographic Instruction Section. rev. ed. Chicago: Association of College and Research Libraries, 1985. (ERIC Document Reproduction Service No. ED 255232).

A061. Blazek, Ron. "The Administrative Climate for Bibliographic Instruction in Large Academic Libraries." Reference Librarian 10 (Summer 1984): 161-79.

A062. Blazek, Ron. "Effective Bibliographic Instruction Programs: a comparison of coordinators and reference heads in ARL libraries." RQ 24 (Summer 1985): 433-41.

A063. Blume, J. Instruction in Catalog Use. Chicago: University of Chicago, 1975.

A064. Bodi, S. "Relevance in Library Instruction: the pursuit." College & Research Libraries 45 (January 1984): 59-65.

Package? Report: encouraging." Library Association Record 80 (June 1978): 279-81.

A102. Clark, Daphne and Others. The Travelling Workshops Experiment in Library User Education. London: British Library, 1981.

A103. Cohen, David. Library Skills. A Self-Paced Program in the Use of Stockton State College Library. Workbook, Handbook, and Program. Pomona, New Jersey: Stockton State College, 1982. (ERIC Document Reproduction Service No. ED 253226).

A104. Coleman, Kathleen. "Library Instruction and the Advancement of Reference Service." Reference Librarian 10 (Summer 1984): 241-52.

A105. Collins, J. "Student Library Use - a matter of encouragement." West Virginia Libraries 31 (Winter 1978): 19-21.

A106. A Comprehensive Program of User Education for the General Libraries: the University of Texas at Austin. (Contributions to Librarianship: no. 1). Austin, Tex.: University of Texas at Austin. General Libraries, 1977.

A107. Coniglio, J. W. "Bibliographic Counseling: the term paper advisory service." Show-Me Libraries 36 (October-November 1984): 79-82.

A108. Connole, T. "Some Tips on Library Orientation." Colorado Libraries 6 (December 1980): 43.

A109. Coons, Bill. INFOQUEST: a research strategy approach to locating information. Logan, Utah: Utah State University, Merrill Library and Learning Resources Program, 1983. (ERIC Document Reproduction Service No. ED 237101).

A110. Cooper, Noele P. "Library Instruction at a University-based Information Center: the informative interview." Research Quarterly 15 (Spring 1976): 233-240.

A111. Costa, Joseph J. Comp. A Directory of Library Instruction Programs in Pennsylvania Academic Libraries. Pittsburgh, Pennsylvania: Pennsylvania Library Association, 1980. (ERIC Document Reproduction Service No. ED 200225).

A065. Bodner, Deborah Huntington. "CLR-NEH Library Programs." North Carolina Libraries 36 (Summer 1978): 3-10.

A066. Bodner, Deborah Huntington. A Descriptive Analysis of the Council on Library Resources' College-Library Programs. Paper for the School of Library Science of the University of North Carolina, 1975.

A067. Boisse, J. A. "Selling Library Instruction." Southeastern Librarian 29 (Summer 1979): 81-5.

A068. Bolner, Mary, ed. Planning and Developing a Library Orientation Program: Proceedings. Papers presented at the Third Annual Conference on Library Orientation for Academic Libraries, Eastern Michigan University, May 3-4, 1973. (Library Orientation Series: No. 3). Published for the Center of Educational Resources, Eastern Michigan University. Ann Arbor, Mich.: Pierian, 1975.

A069. Bopp, R. E. and Van Der Laan, S. J. "Finding Statistical Data." Research Strategies 3 (Spring 1985): 81-6.

A070. Bowen, A. M. "On-line Literature Retrieval as a Continuing Medical Education Course." Medical Library Association Bulletin 65 (July 1977): 384-6.

A071. Bracken, J. and others."Online Searching and Chemistry Students at Knox." College & Research Libraries News 2 (Feburary 1982): 53-4.

A072. Bradfield, V. J. and others. "Librarians or Academics? User Education at Leicester Polytechnic." Aslib Proceedings 29 (March 1977): 133-42.

A073. Brand, M. and Robertson, A. "Literature of Chemistry; a cooperative project." Sci-Tech News 32 (July 1978): 56-7.

A074. Brecht, A. "Accelerated Legal Research at USC [University of Southern California] Law Center." Law Library Journal 75 (Winter 1982): 167-70.

A075. Breem, W. W. S. "Reader Instruction and the Law at Buckingham." Law Librarian 8 (August 1977): 28.

A076. Breivik, Patricia Senn. "Leadership, Management, and the Teaching Library." Library Journal 103 (October 1978): 2045-8.

A077. Breivik, Patricia Senn. Open Admissions and the
      Academic Library. Chicago: American Library
      Association, 1977.

A078. Brewer, J. G. and Hills, P. J. "Evaluation of Reader
      Instruction." Libri 26 (March 1976): 55-66.

A079. Bristow, T. Library Learning: the way to self-help in
      education. London: University of London, Institution
      of Education Library, 1977.

A080. Brundin, Robert E. "Education for Instructional
      Librarians: development and overview." Journal of
      Education for Library and Information Science 25
      (Winter 1985): 177-89.

A081. Bryson, J. A. "Library Orientation and Instruction in
      North Carolina Academic Libraries." North Carolina
      Libraries 33 (Summer-Fall 1975): 19-23.

A082. Budd, J. "Librarians are Teachers." Library Journal 107
      (October 15, 1982): 1944-6.

A083. Buddy, J. W. "Orientation to the University Library
      -- The Missing Link." NASSP Bulletin 66 (December
      1982): 99-102.

A084. Bull, G. E. "Legal Research Education in the UK."
      International Journal of Law Libraries 6 (November
      1978): 237-61.

A085. Bynon, G. E. and McConnell, T. S. "Tour-It-Yourself
      Orientation." Instructional Innovator 25 (May 1980):
      22-3.

A086. Byrd, Patricia; Drum, Carol A.; and Wittkopf,
      Barbara J. Guide to Academic Libraries in the United
      States: for students of English as a second language.
      Englewood Cliffs, NJ.: Prentice-Hall, 1981.

A087. Byrne, F. "Undergraduate Library Instruction at
      Columbia." Bookmark 38 (Fall 1979): 253-6.

A088. Cable, C. L. G. "Object, the Signal, the
      Information." Research Strategies 2 (Spring 1984):
      60-4.

A089. Cage, A. C. "User Education." Texas Library Journal
      61 (Spring 1985): 8.

A090. Cammack, Floyd M. "Leeward Library Offers
      Licenses." Community & Junior College Jo
      (April 1979): 32-3.

A091. Cammack, Floyd M. and DeCosin, Marri. "Co
      College Library Instruction System." Hawaii
      Association Journal 34 (1977): 11-21.

A092. Cammack, Floyd M., DeCosin, Marri, and R
      Norman. Community College Library Instr
      training for self-reliance in basic libra
      Hamden, Connecticut: Linnet Books, 1979.

A093. Campbell, Douglas G. The Law Book Talks:
      instruction for use of legal materia
      undergraduates and the law book talks: a vid
      script. Oshkosh, Wisconsin: Wisconsin Unive
      1984. (ERIC Document Reproduction Service
      254253).

A094. Carey, Kevin. A Study of Periodical Lite
      Searching at an Urban Research Library: proble
      patterns. ERIC Document Reproduction Service,
      (ERIC Document Reproduction Service No. ED 23265

A095. Carlson, David and Miller, Ruth H. "Libraria
      Teaching Faculty: partners in bibliogr
      instruction." College & Research Librari
      (November 1984): 483-91.

A096. Carlson, R. and Others. "Innovations in
      Bibliographic Instruction." Law Library Jourr
      (Summer 1981): 615-8.

A097. Carson, J. "Bibliographic Instruction: explorin
      new technology for library instruction." Coll
      Research Libraries News 9 (October 1983): 337.

A098. Cheetham, D. L. "Viewpoint [on library instructic
      Art Libraries Journal 3 (Winter 1978): 2-4.

A099. Cipolla, K. G. "M.I.T's Point-Of-Use Concept: a f
      year update." Journal of Academic Librariansh
      (January 1980): 326-8.

A100. Clark, A. S. and Evans, A. "Slide/Tape Introduc
      to a Research Library: Ohio State University." C
      Library Association Bulletin 45 (January 1975): 33.

A101. Clark, D. and Harris, C. "Can Users Be Instructe

A065. Bodner, Deborah Huntington. "CLR-NEH Library Programs." North Carolina Libraries 36 (Summer 1978): 3-10.

A066. Bodner, Deborah Huntington. A Descriptive Analysis of the Council on Library Resources' College-Library Programs. Paper for the School of Library Science of the University of North Carolina, 1975.

A067. Boisse, J. A. "Selling Library Instruction." Southeastern Librarian 29 (Summer 1979): 81-5.

A068. Bolner, Mary, ed. Planning and Developing a Library Orientation Program: Proceedings. Papers presented at the Third Annual Conference on Library Orientation for Academic Libraries, Eastern Michigan University, May 3-4, 1973. (Library Orientation Series: No. 3). Published for the Center of Educational Resources, Eastern Michigan University. Ann Arbor, Mich.: Pierian, 1975.

A069. Bopp, R. E. and Van Der Laan, S. J. "Finding Statistical Data." Research Strategies 3 (Spring 1985): 81-6.

A070. Bowen, A. M. "On-line Literature Retrieval as a Continuing Medical Education Course." Medical Library Association Bulletin 65 (July 1977): 384-6.

A071. Bracken, J. and others."Online Searching and Chemistry Students at Knox." College & Research Libraries News 2 (Feburary 1982): 53-4.

A072. Bradfield, V. J. and others. "Librarians or Academics? User Education at Leicester Polytechnic." Aslib Proceedings 29 (March 1977): 133-42.

A073. Brand, M. and Robertson, A. "Literature of Chemistry; a cooperative project." Sci-Tech News 32 (July 1978): 56-7.

A074. Brecht, A. "Accelerated Legal Research at USC [University of Southern California] Law Center." Law Library Journal 75 (Winter 1982): 167-70.

A075. Breem, W. W. S. "Reader Instruction and the Law at Buckingham." Law Librarian 8 (August 1977): 28.

A076. Breivik, Patricia Senn. "Leadership, Management, and the Teaching Library." Library Journal 103 (October 1978): 2045-8.

A077. Breivik, Patricia Senn. Open Admissions and the Academic Library. Chicago: American Library Association, 1977.

A078. Brewer, J. G. and Hills, P. J. "Evaluation of Reader Instruction." Libri 26 (March 1976): 55-66.

A079. Bristow, T. Library Learning: the way to self-help in education. London: University of London, Institution of Education Library, 1977.

A080. Brundin, Robert E. "Education for Instructional Librarians: development and overview." Journal of Education for Library and Information Science 25 (Winter 1985): 177-89.

A081. Bryson, J. A. "Library Orientation and Instruction in North Carolina Academic Libraries." North Carolina Libraries 33 (Summer-Fall 1975): 19-23.

A082. Budd,J. "Librarians are Teachers." Library Journal 107 (October 15, 1982): 1944-6.

A083. Buddy, J. W. "Orientation to the University Library -- The Missing Link." NASSP Bulletin 66 (December 1982): 99-102.

A084. Bull, G. E. "Legal Research Education in the UK." International Journal of Law Libraries 6 (November 1978): 237-61.

A085. Bynon, G. E. and McConnell, T. S. "Tour-It-Yourself Orientation." Instructional Innovator 25 (May 1980): 22-3.

A086. Byrd, Patricia; Drum, Carol A.; and Wittkopf, Barbara J. Guide to Academic Libraries in the United States: for students of English as a second language. Englewood Cliffs, NJ.: Prentice-Hall, 1981.

A087. Byrne, F. "Undergraduate Library Instruction at Columbia." Bookmark 38 (Fall 1979): 253-6.

A088. Cable, C. L. G. "Object, the Signal, the Information." Research Strategies 2 (Spring 1984): 60-4.

A089. Cage, A. C. "User Education." Texas Library Journal 61 (Spring 1985): 8.

A090. Cammack, Floyd M. "Leeward Library Offers Learning Licenses." Community & Junior College Journal 49 (April 1979): 32-3.

A091. Cammack, Floyd M. and DeCosin, Marri. "Community College Library Instruction System." Hawaii Library Association Journal 34 (1977): 11-21.

A092. Cammack, Floyd M., DeCosin, Marri, and Roberts, Norman. Community College Library Instruction: training for self-reliance in basic library use. Hamden, Connecticut: Linnet Books, 1979.

A093. Campbell, Douglas G. The Law Book Talks: library instruction for use of legal materials by undergraduates and the law book talks: a video tape script. Oshkosh, Wisconsin: Wisconsin University, 1984. (ERIC Document Reproduction Service No. ED 254253).

A094. Carey, Kevin. A Study of Periodical Literature Searching at an Urban Research Library: problems and patterns. ERIC Document Reproduction Service, 1982. (ERIC Document Reproduction Service No. ED 232652).

A095. Carlson, David and Miller, Ruth H. "Librarians and Teaching Faculty: partners in bibliographic instruction." College & Research Libraries 45 (November 1984): 483-91.

A096. Carlson, R. and Others. "Innovations in Legal Bibliographic Instruction." Law Library Journal 74 (Summer 1981): 615-8.

A097. Carson, J. "Bibliographic Instruction: exploring the new technology for library instruction." College & Research Libraries News 9 (October 1983): 337.

A098. Cheetham, D. L. "Viewpoint [on library instruction]." Art Libraries Journal 3 (Winter 1978): 2-4.

A099. Cipolla, K. G. "M.I.T's Point-Of-Use Concept: a five-year update." Journal of Academic Librarianship 5 (January 1980): 326-8.

A100. Clark, A. S. and Evans, A. "Slide/Tape Introduction to a Research Library: Ohio State University." Ohio Library Association Bulletin 45 (January 1975): 33.

A101. Clark, D. and Harris, C. "Can Users Be Instructed by

Package? Report: encouraging." Library Association
Record 80 (June 1978): 279-81.

A102. Clark, Daphne and Others. The Travelling Workshops
Experiment in Library User Education. London: British
Library, 1981.

A103. Cohen, David. Library Skills. A Self-Paced Program in
the Use of Stockton State College Library. Workbook,
Handbook, and Program. Pomona, New Jersey: Stockton
State College, 1982. (ERIC Document Reproduction
Service No. ED 253226).

A104. Coleman, Kathleen. "Library Instruction and the
Advancement of Reference Service." Reference
Librarian 10 (Summer 1984): 241-52.

A105. Collins, J. "Student Library Use - a matter of
encouragement." West Virginia Libraries 31 (Winter
1978): 19-21.

A106. A Comprehensive Program of User Education for the
General Libraries: the University of Texas at Austin.
(Contributions to Librarianship: no. 1). Austin, Tex.:
University of Texas at Austin. General Libraries,
1977.

A107. Coniglio, J. W. "Bibliographic Counseling: the term
paper advisory service." Show-Me Libraries 36
(October-November 1984): 79-82.

A108. Connole, T. "Some Tips on Library Orientation."
Colorado Libraries 6 (December 1980): 43.

A109. Coons, Bill. INFOQUEST: a research strategy approach
to locating information. Logan, Utah: Utah State
University, Merrill Library and Learning Resources
Program, 1983. (ERIC Document Reproduction Service
No. ED 237101).

A110. Cooper, Noele P. "Library Instruction at a
University-based Information Center: the informative
interview." Research Quarterly 15 (Spring 1976): 233-
240.

A111. Costa, Joseph J. Comp. A Directory of Library
Instruction Programs in Pennsylvania Academic
Libraries. Pittsburgh, Pennsylvania: Pennsylvania
Library Association, 1980. (ERIC Document
Reproduction Service No. ED 200225).

A112. Cottam, K. M. and Dowell, C. V. "Conceptual Planning Method for Developing Bibliographic Instruction Programs." Journal of Academic Librarianship 7 (September 1981): 223-8.

A113. "Council on Library Resources Has Awarded a Three-Year Grant of $42,771 to the Library Orientation-Instruction Exchange (LOEX) at Eastern Michigan University." Library of Congress Information Bulletin 34 (Feburary 7, 1975): 57.

A114. Cravey, P. J. "User and Bibliographic Instruction in the Academic Library." Georgia Librarian 16 (Feburary 1979): 12.

A115. Crimmins, Mary E. and Others. Northern Illinois University Libraries. Library Instruction: scope and mission statement. Dekalb, Illinois: Northern Illinois University Libraries, 1979. (ERIC Document Reproduction Service No. ED 250007).

A116. Culley, J. D. and Others. "Business Students and the University Library: an overlooked element in the business curriculum." Journal of Academic Librarianship 2 (January 1977): 293-6.

A117. Dane, Jean and Thomas, Philip A. How to Use a Law Library. London: Sweet & Maxwell, 1979.

A118. Dantin, Doris B. Comp. Bibliographic Instruction Programs in Louisiana Academic Libraries: a directory. Louisiana: Louisiana Library Association, 1983.

A119. Dash, U. "Self-Guided Library Tour." Australia Academic and Research Libraries 8 (March 1977): 33-8.

A120. Daugherty, Robert. "Instructing Patrons in OCLC in an Academic Library." College & Research Libraries News 2 (Feburary 1983): 35.

A121. Daugherty, Robert. "Operational Ramifications of LCS: user education." Illinois Libraries 64 (January 1982): 44-6.

A122. Daugherty, Robert and Pausch, Lois M. Bibliographic Instruction in Illinois Academic Libraries: a survey report. (Illinois Library Statistical Report No. 11.) Springfield, Illinois: Illinois State Library, 1983. (ERIC Document Reproduction Service No. ED 238454).

A123. Davidson, N. "Bibliographic Instruction Roundup." South Carolina Librarian 28 (Fall 1984): 18-9.

A124. Davidson, N. "Bits, Bytes and Bibliographic Instruction; Orientation/Instruction Round-Up." [two conferences held this spring]. South Carolina Librarian 27 (Fall 1983): 17-9.

A125. Davidson, N. "Government Documents: an integrated part of the BI program in Colleges." South Carolina Librarian 28 (Spring 1984): 19-20.

A126. Davis, Elisabeth B.; Northrup, Diana E.; Self, Phyllis C.; and Williams, Mitsuko. "A Two-Phased Model for Library Instruction." Bulletin of the Medical Library Association 65 (January 1977): 40-5.

A127. Davis, H. L. and Weddle, K. S. "Prepare now for CUD Workshop; user education in academic libraries." Oklahoma Librarian 25 (October 1975): 24-6.

A128. Davis, H. Scott. An Introduction to Your College Library: making it work for you. ERIC Document Reproduction Service, 1984. (ERIC Document Reproduction Service No. ED 253254).

A129. De Lerma, Dominique-Rene. Involvement With Music: resources for music research. New York: Harper's College Press, 1977.

A130. Delgado, H. B. R. "Humanizing Function of the College Library; or, Providing Students With Library Know-How." Catholic Library World 49 (Feburary 1978): 278-81.

A131. Delgado, H. B. R. ed. Library Instruction In the Seventies: state of the art. Papers presented at the sixth annual Conference on Library Orientation for Academic Libraries held at Eastern Michigan University May 13-14, 1976. Michigan: Pierian, 1977.

A132. Delgado, H. B. R. "Library Orientation and Instruction, 1975; an annotated review of the literature." Ohio Association of School Librarians Bulletin 28 (October 1976): 18-25.

A133. Delgado, H. B. R. "Library Orientation and Instruction, 1976; an annotated review of the literature." Reference Services Review 5 (January 1977): 41-4.

A134. Delgado, H. B. R. "Library Orientation and Instruction, 1977; an annotated review of the literature." Reference Services Review 6 (January 1978): 45-51.

A135. Delgado, H. B. R. "Library Orientation and Instruction 1978; an annotated review of the literature." Reference Services Review 7 (January 1979): 45-56.

A136. De Loach, M. L. and Morgan, E. A. "Reference and Information Services in the Small Academic Library." Bookmark 41 (Winter 1983): 85-90.

A137. Derksen, C. R. M. and Ward, S. N. "Removing Barriers to the Use of Geologic Maps for Non-Geologists." Bulletin (Special Libraries Assocication. Geography and Map Division) No. 139 (March 1985): 2-9.

A138. Deshpande, K. S. "User Orientation in College Libraries in India." Library Science with a Slant to Documentation 15 (December 1978): 191-5.

A139. Devine, Marie E. Guide to Library Research. A Basic Text for the Undergraduate. 2nd ed. Asheville, North Carolina: University of North Carolina.Ramsey Library. (ERIC Document Reproduction Service No. ED 258578).

A140. Dickinson, D. W. "Library Literacy: who? when? where?" Library Journal 106 (April 15, 1981): 853-5.

A141. Dillon, H. W. "Organizing the Academic Library for Instruction." Journal of Academic Librarianship 1 (September 1975): 4-7.

A142. Diskin, G. M. and Michalak, T. J. "Beyond the Online Catalog: Utilizing the OPAC for Library Information." Library Hi Tech 3 No. 1 (1985): 7-13.

A143. "Dissertations in Bibliographic Instruction." Research Strategies 2 (Summer 1984): 149-52.

A144. Dittmar, Jeanne. Library Service Enhancement Program, F. W. Crumb Memorial Library, State University College, Postdam, New York. Final Report. Potsdam, New York: State University of New York, Postdam, F. W. Crumb Memorial Library, 1977. (ERIC Document Reproduction Service No. ED 157554).

A145. Doelker, Richard F. and Toifel, P. "The Development
of a Self-Guided, Library-Based Materials and Methods
Manual for Social Work Research." Behavioral and
Social Sciences Librarian 3 (Summer 1984): 81-93.

A146. Dougherty, R. M. "Avoiding Burnout [relationship
between bibliographic instruction and reference
work]." Journal of Academic Librarianship 7 (January
1982): 333.

A147. Dougherty, R. M. and Webb, W. H. "Editorial: library
instruction." Journal of Academic Librarianship 2
(September 1976): 171.

A148. Douglas, Nancy E. and Baum, Nathan. Library Research
Guide to Psychology: illustrated search strategy and
sources. ("Library Research Guides" Series, no. 7).
Ann Arbor, Mich.: Pierian, 1984.

A149. Downing, A. "Evaluating Bibliographic Instruction."
New Jersey Libraries 15 (Fall 1982): 18-21.

A150. Downs, Robert Bingham and Keller, Clara D. How to Do
Library Research. 2nd ed. Urbana, Ill.: University of
Illinois Press, 1975.

A151. Doyen, S. E. "Study of Library Skills Instruction."
Top of the News 38 (Fall 1981): 60-3.

A152. Drabek, T. E. and Others. "Query Analysis System: a
new tool for increasing the effectiveness of library
utilization by sociology students." Teaching
Sociology 6 (October 1978): 47-68

A153. Dreifuss, Richard A. "Library Instruction and
Graduate Students: more work for George." RQ 21
(Winter 1981): 121-3.

A154. Dreifuss, Richard A. "Library Instruction In the
Database Searching Context." RQ 21 (Spring 1982): 233-
8.

A155. Dresser, S. L. "Bibliographic Instruction: one
librarian's view." Arkansas Libraries 39 (June 1982):
16-7.

A156. Druesedow, John E. Jr. Library Research Guide to
Music: illustrated search strategy and sources.
(Library Research Guides Series, no. 6). Ann Arbor,
Mich.: Pierian, 1982.

A157. Dubin, E. and others. "In Depth Analysis of a Term Paper Clinic." Illinois Libraries 60 (March 1978): 324-33.

A158. Dudley, M. "Teachers and Librarians: partners in library instruction." Catholic Library World 52 (July 1980): 17-21.

A159. Duffill, C. "Library User Education in the Online Age." Australian Academic and Research Libraries 15 (December 1984): 232-3.

A160. Duffill, C. "Strategies for User Education for Graduate Students." IATUL Proceedings 17 (1985): 163-70.

A161. Dyson, A. J. "Organizing Undergraduate Library Instruction: the English and American experience." Journal of Academic Librarianship 1 (March 1975): 9-13.

A162. Eberhart, G. M. "Earlham College Still a Model for Course-Integrated BI." College & Research Libraries News no. 6 (June 1985): 295.

A163. "Educating the User; New Approaches Tried." Library Journal 103 (Feburary 15,1978): 424.

A164. Edwards, J. D. "LEXIS and WESTLAW Instruction in the Law School: University of Oklahoma." Law Library Journal 76 (Summer 1983): 605-31.

A165. Eisenbach, E. "Bibliographic Instruction From the Other Side of the Desk." RQ 17 (Summer 1978): 312-6.

A166. Elkins, Elizabeth A. and Morris, Jacquelyn M. "Bibliographic Instruction in New York Academic Libraries." Bookmark 38 (Fall 1979): 211-8.

A167. Eng, S. "CAI and the Future of Bibliographic Instruction." Catholic Library World 55 (May 1984): 441-4.

A168. Engeldinger, E. A. "Bibliographic Instruction for Study Abroad Programs." College & Research Libraries News No. 8 (September 1985): 395-8.

A169. Engeldinger, E. A. and Stevens, B. R. "Library Instruction Within the Curriculum." College & Research Libraries News 11 (December 1984): 593-4.

A170. Euster, J. R. ed. "Reactions to the Think Tank Recommendations: a symposium." Journal of Academic Librarianship 9 (March 1983): 4-14.

A171. Evaluation Bibliographic Instruction: a handbook. Chicago, Ill.: American Library Association, 1983.

A172. Facinelli, Jaclyn. Music Students and Bibliography Instruction: a study. ERIC Document Reproduction Service, 1982. (ERIC Document Reproduction Service No. ED 242322).

A173. Farber, Evan Ira. "BI and Library Instruction: some observations." Reference Librarian 10 (Spring-Summer 1984): 5-13.

A174. Farber, Evan Ira. "Catalog Dependency." Library Journal 109 (February 15, 1984): 325-8.

A175. Fenner, Peter and Armstrong, Martha C. Research: a practical guide to finding information. Los Altos, CA.: William Kaufmann, 1981.

A176. Figueiredo, Nice. User Education and Marketing of Information Services in Brazil. Paper presented at the Annual Conference of FID/ET (The Hague, Netherlands, September, 1984). ERIC Document Reproduction Service, 1984. (ERIC Document Reproduction Service No. ED 253253).

A177. Fink, D. "Developing an Academic Bibliographic Instruction Program: the dual role of the instruction librarian." Colorado Libraries 9 (June 1983): 22-4.

A178. Finn, David, Ashby, Margaret, and Drury, Susan. A Teaching Manual for Tutor-Librarians. London: Library Association, 1978.

A179. Fjallbrant, Nancy. " A Comparison of User Instruction in Scandinavian and British Academic Libraries." Transactions of Chalmers University of Technology 337 (1975): 1-37.

A180. Fjallbrant, Nancy. "Evaluation of an Introductory Course in Information Retrieval for Engineering Undergraduates by Means of Pre-structured Interviews." Tidskrift for Dokumentation 33 (1977): 87-90.

A181. Fjallbrant, Nancy "Evaluation of Introductory Courses in Information Retrieval at Chalmers University of

Technology Library by Means of Studies of Student Attitudes." Tidskrift for Dokumentation 32 (1976): 109-14.

A182. Fjallbrant, Nancy. "Library-User Education in Japan: recent trends in higher-education institutions." UNESCO Journal of Information Science 5 (October 1983): 243-8.

A183. Fjallbrant, Nancy. "Planning a Programme of Library User Education." Journal of Librarianship 9 (July 1977): 199-211.

A184. Fjallbrant, Nancy. "Teaching Methods for the Education of the Library User." Libri 26 (December 1976): 252-67.

A185. Fjallbrant, Nancy. "User Education and Its Integration Into the Functioning of the Academic Library." Nordisk Tidskrift for Bok-och Biblioteksvasen 64 (1977): 44-51.

A186. Fjallbrant, Nancy. "User Education in Australian Academic Libraries." Education for Information: the international review of education and training in library and information science 1 (September 1983): 191-216.

A187. Fjallbrant, Nancy. "User Education in Swedish Academic Libraries; a survey of recent developments." Libri 32 (September 1982): 224-40.

A188. Fjallbrant, Nancy, ed. User Education in the Online Age. Proceedings of an international Seminar held 17-19 August 1982, Gothenburg, Sweden. Goteborg: IATUL, Chalmers University of Technology Library, 1982.

A189. Fjallbrant, Nancy, ed. User Education in the Online Age II: international seminar 30th July - 2nd August 1984, Delft, The Netherland. Goteborg: IATUL, Chalmers University of Technology Library, 1985.

A190. Fjallbrant, Nancy, ed. User Education in University of Technology Libraries. Goteborg: IATUL, 1977.

A191. Fjallbrant, Nancy. User Education Programmes in Swedish academic libraries: a study of developments in the years 1973-1977. Goteborg: Chalmers Tekniska Hogskola, Biblioteket, 1977.

A192. Fjallbrant, Nancy and Malley, Ian. User Education In Libraries. 2nd rev. ed. London: Clive Bingley, 1984.

A193. Fjallbrant, Nancy and Others. "End-user Training in the Use of a Small Swedish Database." College & Research Libraries 44 (March 1983): 161-7.

A194. Fjallbrant, Nancy and Others. "Self-Paced Exercises for Library Orientation." Aslib Proceedings 33 (June 1981): 251-6.

A195. Fjallbrant, Nancy and Stevenson, Malcolm B. User Education in Libraries: problems and practice. Hamden, Conn.: Linnet Books, 1978.

A196. Ford, James E. "The Natural Alliance Between Librarians and English Teachers in Course-Related Library Use Instruction." College & Research Libraries 43 (September 1982): 379-84.

A197. Foreman, G. E. and Mueller, M. H. "A Credit Course For Medical Students." Medical Reference Services Querterly 4 (Fall 1985): 61-66.

A198. "Forum: bibliographic instruction." Tennessee Librarian 32 (Summer 1980): 13-7; (Fall 1980): 35-7.

A199. Foster, B. "Hunter Midtown Library: the closing of an open door." Journal of Academic Librarianship 2 (November 1976): 235-7.

A200. Foster, Jocelyn H. "Influence Through User Education -- a strategy for campus librarians." Canadian Library Journal 38 (Feburary 1981): 35-7.

A201. Fox, Peter, ed. Library User Education: are new approaches needed? Proceedings of a conference, Trinity College, Cambridge, 1979. Research and Development Report no. 5503. London: British Library, 1980.

A202. Franco, Elaine A., ed. Improving the Use of Libraries. Proceedings from the Spring Meeting of the Nebraska Library Association, College and University Section (Peru, Nebraska, April 14-5, 1983). Lincoln, Nebraska: Nebraska Library Association, 1983. (ERIC Document Reproduction Service No. ED 234817).

A203. Franco, Elaine A., ed. Proceedings from the 1982

Spring Meeting of the Nebraska Library Association, College and University Section (Seward, Nebraska, April 15-6, 1982). Lincoln, Nebraska: Nebraska Library Association, 1982. (ERIC Document Reproduction Service No. ED 231359).

A204. Frank, V. and Trzebiatowski, Elaine. "Designing Search Strategies: an Approach to Library Instruction." Illinois Libraries 63 (October 1981): 573-7.

A205. Freedman, Janet L. and Bantly, Harold A., comps. Information Searching: a handbook for designing and creating instructional programs. Rev. ed. Metuchen, NJ.: Scarecrow, 1982.

A206. Freeman, M. S. "Published Study Guides: what they say about libraries." Journal of Academic Librarianship 5 (November 1979): 252-5.

A207. Freides, Thelma. "Current Trends in Academic Libraries." Library Trends 31 (Winter 1983): 457-74.

A208. "Freshman English Teachers and Librarians at the University of Arizona Have Joined In An Effort To Equip New Students With That Necessary Skill: how to use a university library." College & Research Libraries News 11 (December 1977): 332.

A209. Frick, E. "Humanizing Technology Through Instruction." [Presented at the CLA Annual Conference, 1984.] Canadian Library Journal 41 (October 1984): 263-7.

A210. Frick, E. "Information Structure and Bibliographic Instruction." Journal of Academic Librarianship 1 (September 1975): 12-4.

A211. Frick, Elizabeth. Library Research Guide to History: illustrated search strategy and sources. ("Library Research Guides" Series, no. 4). Ann Arbor, Mich.: Pierian, 1980.

A212. Fry, T. K. "Bibliographic Instruction: user education at UCLA." College & Research Libraries News no. 9 (October 1982): 317+.

A213. Fryman, James F. and Wilkinson, Patrick J. "Federal Statistics: teaching the basics to Geography students." Journal of Geography 84 (May-June 1985): 128-30.

A214. Galloway, Sue. "Nobody Is Teaching the Teachers."
Booklegger Magazine 3 (January/February 1976): 29-31.

A215. Galloway, Sue, and Sherwood, Virginia. "Essentials
for an Academic Library's Instructional Service
Program." California Librarian 37 (April 1976): 44-9.

A216. Ganz, C. "Education and Training for the User and the
Information Specialist: an overview." Library Science
with a Slant to Documentation 15 (June 1978): 67-71.

A217. Gates, Jean Key. Guide to the Use of Books and
Libraries. 4th ed. New York: McGraw-Hill, 1979.

A218. Gates, Jean Key. Guide to the Use of Libraries and
Information Sources. 5th ed. New York: McGraw-Hill,
1983.

A219. George, Mary W. and Hogan, Sharon A. "Information on
Cards and What It All Means." Research Strategies 2
(Spring 1984): 88-97.

A220. Getchell, C. M. "Bibliographic Instruction: a non-
credit/non-graded course at the University of Kansas."
College & Research Libraries News no. 6 (June 1981):
173-4.

A221. Getting There From Here: a library skills workshop.
rev. ed. NY.: SUNY, College at Brockport, Drake
Memorial Library, 1982.

A222. Gibson, C. E. and Smith, H. B.   "Increasing End-user
Awareness of Library Services Through Promotion:
Grumman Aerospace Corporation." Science & Technology
Libraries 5 (Fall 1984): 69-77.

A223. Gillispie, J. "Library Instruction in a Map Library
Via Slide/Tape." SLA Geography and Map Division
Bulletin No. 131 (March 1983): 2-13.

A224. Gilmer, L. C. "Bibliographic Instruction and
Continuing Education." College & Research Libraries
News No. 6 (June 1982): 201-2.

A225. Glogoff, Stuart. "Using Statistical Tests to Evaluate
Library Instruction Sessions." Journal of Academic
Librarianship 4 (January 1979): 38-42.

A226. Glogoff, Stuart and Seeds, Robert A. "Interest Among
Librarians to Participate in Library-Related

Instruction at the Pennsylvania State University Libraries." Pennsylvania Library Association Bulletin 31 (May 1976): 55-6.

A227. Goudy, Frank Wm. and Moushey, Eugene. "Library Instruction and Foreign Students: a survey of opinions and practices among selected libraries." Reference Librarian No. 10 Part 2 (Spring-Summer 1984): 15-26.

A228. Gover, Harvey R. Keys to Library Research on the Graduate Level: a guide to guides. Washington, D.C.: University Press of America, 1981.

A229. "Graduate Bibliographic Instruction in the University of Michigan Library." Journal of Academic Librarianship 1 (May 1975): 24-5.

A230. Graham, Christine. ed. Library Resources. A Self-Paced Workbook. 3rd. ed. San Francisco, California: San Francisco State University, Leonard Library, 1983. (ERIC Document Reproduction Service No. ED 248899).

A231. Gratch, B. "Trivializing Your Library [trivia contest in the dorm dining halls for BI promotion]." College & Research Libraries News 7 (July 1984): 341-2.

A232. Greenberg, Bette. How to Find Out in Psychiatry: a guide to sources of mental health information New York: Pergamon, 1978.

A233. Greenfield, Louise and Others. University of Arizona Library. A Final Report from the Public Services Research Projects. Assessing the Instructional Needs of Students in a Selected Scientific Discipline at the University of Arizona. One of a Series of Self-Studies and Research Projects. Tucson, Arizona: Arizona University Library, 1985. (ERIC Document Reproduction Service No. ED 255225).

A234. Greig, J. S. and Others. "Reader Education for Engineers: a progress report." Australian Academic and Research Libraries 6 (September 1975): 133-4.

A235. Gwinn, N. E. "Academic Libraries and Undergraduate Education: the CLR experience." College & Research Libraries 41 (January 1980): 5-16.

A236. Gwinn, N. E. "Faculty-Library Connection." Change 10 (September 1978): 19-21.

A237. Haarala, A. R. "Training for Online Information: automation, libraries, users and the future." IATUL Proceedings 17 (1985): 97-102.

A238. Hales, Celia and Catlett, D. "The Credit Course: reaffirmation from two university libraries: methodology; East Carolina University." Research Strategies 2 (Fall 1984): 156-65.

A239. Hales, Celia and Others. Strategies for Searching. A Self-Paced Workbook for Basic Library Skills. 2nd ed. ERIC Document Reproduction Service, 1984. (ERIC Document Reproduction Service No. ED 252228).

A240. Hall, V. B. and Others. "Slide-tape Program for Beginning Pharmacy Students: effect on learning." Medical Library Association Bulletin 65 (October 1977): 443-5.

A241. Hall, V. S. "Access to Reference Tools of Geological Literature Via the Carramate; an individual teaching tool." Kentucky Library Association Bulletin 39 no. 4 (1975): 27-9.

A242. Hall, V. S. "Bibliographic Instruction: a new role for the special librarian." Kentucky Libraries 45 (Fall 1981): 8-13.

A243. Hallman, Clark N. A Library Instruction Program for Beginning Undergraduates. Omaha, Nebraska: Nebraska University, University Library, 1980. (ERIC Document Reproduction Service No. ED 188633).

A244. Haltiwanger, A. A. "Treasure Hunt Library Orientation." Unabashed Librarian no. 4 (1982): 22.

A245. Hamilton, F. and Turner, S. J. "Bibliographic Instruction: just formalizing a trend?" Mississippi Libraries 43 (Summer 1979): 97-8.

A246. Hansen, F. and Lee, J H. "Ancient Greek History as a Library Instruction Course." Research Strategies 3 (Spring 1985): 65-74.

A247. Hanson, J. R. "Teaching Information Sources in Business Studies: an application of the theories of J. Bruner and R. M. Gagne." Journal of Librarianship (July 1985): 185-99.

A248. Hardesty, Larry. Bibliographic Instruction: defining,

organizing, and promoting a program. ERIC Document
Reproduction Service, 1977. (ERIC Document
Reproduction Service No. ED 163892).

A249. Hardesty, Larry. "Use of Slide-Tape Presentations in
Academic Libraries: a state-of-the-art survey."
Journal of Academic Librarianship 3 (July 1977): 137-
40.

A250. Hardesty, Larry and Others. "Evaluating Library-Use
Instruction." College & Research Libraries 40 (July
1979): 309-17.

A251. Hardesty, Larry and Others. "Library-Use
Instruction: assessment of the long-term effects."
College & Research Libraries 43 (January 1982): 38-46.

A252. Hardesty, Larry and Wright, J. "Student Library
Skills and Attitudes and Their Change: relationships
to other selected variables." Journal of Academic
Librarianship 8 (September 1982): 216-20.

A253. Harris, C. "Educating the User: travelling workshops
experiment." Library Association Record 79 (July
1977): 359-60.

A254. Harris, C. "Project Methods and the Need for Library
User Instruction." Assistant Librarian 71 (July-August
1978): 78-80.

A255. Hart, J. W. "Continuing Education Update." College &
Research Libraries News 5 (May 1984): 236-7.

A256. Hatchard, D. B. and Toy, P. "Evaluation of a Library
Instruction Programme at BCAE [Bendigo College of
Advanced Education]." Australian Academic and
Research Libraries 15 (September 1984): 157-67.

A257. Hatchard, D. B. and Toy, P. "Incoming Students and
the Academic Library." Australian Academic and
Research Libraries 15 (March, 1984): 23-8.

A258. Hatt, F. "Library Instruction, Individualized Learning
and Independent Learnings." Art Library Journal 3
(Winter 1978): 5-16.

A259. Hauer, Mary G., Murray, Ruth C., Dantin, Doris B.,
and Bolner, Myrtle S. Books, Libraries, and Research.
2nd ed. Dubuque, Iowa: Kendall and Hunt, 1983.

A260. Hazen, D. C. "Ideology of Outreach: library instruction and the academy." Cornell University Libraries Bulletin 209 (July 1978): 20-4.

A261. Head, S. L. Evaluation of the Library Skills Course at the University of Missouri, Columbia. Columbia, Missouri: University of Missouri, 1980.

A262. Hernon, P. "Instruction in the Use of Academic Libraries: a preliminary study of the early years as based on selective extant materials." Journal of Library History, Philosophy & Comparative Librarianship 17 (Winter 1982): 16-38.

A263. Hernon, P. "Library Lectures and Their Evaluation: a survey." Journal of Academic Librarianship 1 (July 1975): 14-8.

A264. Hicks, Joan Tomay. "Computer-Assisted Instruction in Library Orientation and Services." Bulletin of the Medical Library Association 64 (April 1976): 238-240.

A265. Hills, P. J. "Self-Teaching and the Development of the Individual." Aslib Proceedings 28 (September 1976): 305-13.

A266. Hills, P. J. "Tape/Slide to Teaching Package: the place of the SCONUL Tape/Slide Scheme in Educating the Library User." IATUL Proceedings 9 (1977): 23-9.

A267. Hills, P. J. ed. Tape Slide Presentations and Teaching Packages for Library User Education. London: Standing Conference of National and University Libraries, 1977.

A268. Hills, P. J., Lincoln, L., and Turner, L. P. Evaluation of Tape-Slide Guides for Library Instruction. (British Library Research and Development Reports). London, Eng.: British Library, 1978.

A269. Hobbins, J. "Challenge to Teach: instruction in academic libraries." Argus 5 (May-August 1976): 44.

A270. Hofmann, L. A. "Educate the Educator: a possible solution to an academic librarian's dilemma." Journal of Academic Librarianship 7 (July 1981): 161-3.

A271. Homick, Ronald J. "Library Use Instruction in Community Colleges." Catholic Library World 55 (April 1984): 398-401.

A272. Hopkins, F. L. "Century of Bibliographic Instruction: the hostorical claim to professional and academic legitimacy." College & Research Libraries 43 (May 1982): 192-8.

A273. Hopkinson, S. L. Instructional Material for Teaching the Use of the Library; a selective, annotated bibliography of films, filmstrips, books and pamphlets, tests and other aids. 5th ed. San Jose, California: Claremont House, 1975.

A274. Horton, J. S. "A Never Ending Battle: students and library skills." Indiana Media Journal 7 (Spring 1985): 12-4.

A275. Horton, J. S. "Library Skills in College: the heritage of high school." Indiana Media Journal 1 (Spring 1979): 19-20.

A276. Horton, W. J. Relationship of Library Skills to the Use of the Library by Freshman Community College Students. Texas: North Texas State University, 1979.

A277. Houghton, B. "Whatever Happened to Tutor Librarianship?" Art Library Journal 1 (Winter 1976): 4-19.

A278. Howard, Sheila. "Library Use Education for Adult University Students." Canadian Library Journal 40 (June 1983): 149-55.

A279. Howery, C. B. "BI for Sociologists." College & Research Libraries News no. 8 (September 1982): 278.

A280. Hsu, M. "Library Orientation for Undergraduates: a new look." Cornell University Library Bulletin no. 202 (October 1976): 16-8.

A281. Huber, K. and Lewis, P. "Tired of Term Papers? Options for Librarians and Professors." Research Strategies 2 (Fall 1984): 192-9.

A282. Hughes, Phyllis and Flandreau, Arthur. "Tutorial Library Instruction: the freshman program at Berea College." Journal of Academic Librarianship 6 (May 1980): 91-4.

A283. Ishaq, M. R. and Cornick, D. P. "Library and Research Consultations (LaRC): a service for graduate students." RQ 18 (Winter 1978): 168-76.

A284. Iyengar, T. K. S. "User Orientation in University Libraries." Library Science with a Slant to Documentation 15 (December 1978): 177-82.

A285. Jackson, W. J. "User Education [Library Guides at the University of Houston]." Texas Library Journal 60 (Summer 1984): 58-60.

A286. Jackson, W. J. "User-friendly Library Guide." College & Research Libraries News 9 (October 1984): 468-71.

A287. Jackson, W. J. "The User-Friendly Library Guide." Show-Me Libraries 36 (October-November 1984): 75-8.

A288. Jacobs, James A. and Baber, Carolyn D. Report of the Ad Hoc User Instruction Committee, Texas Tech University Library. Final Revision. Lubbock, Texas: Texas Tech University, 1984. (ERIC Document Reproduction Service No. ED 254234).

A289. Jacobson, Eric. How to Use a Law Library. Los Angeles, California: Constitutional Rights Foundation, 1977.

A290. Jacobson, F. E. "Bibliographic Instruction — Again." Colorado Libraries 7 (March 1981): 36-7.

A291. Jacobson, G. N. and Albright, M. J. "Motivation via Videotape: key to undergraduate library instruction in the research library." Journal of Academic Librarianship 9 (November 1983):270-5.

A292. Jamieson, D. G. and Simpson, I. A. "Reader Instruction in the Health Sciences at Otago." New Zealand Libraries 41 (December 1978): 110-3.

A293. Jaramillo, G. R. "Educating the Library User: a survey of academic libraries in Colorado." Colorado Libraries 9 (June 1983): 18-21.

A294. Jay, H. L. "Why Hasn't Anyone Told Me This Before?" SLJ 31 (March 1985): 124.

A295. Jean, Lorraine A. Introducing the College-Bound Student to the Academic Library: a case study. Dekalb, Illinois: Northern Illinois University Libraries, 1981. (ERIC Document Reproduction Service No. ED 200236).

A296. Jeffries, J. "TV Can Teach Readers Best." Library Association Record 78 (January 1976): 18.

A297. Jennerich, E. Z. and Smith, B. H. "Bibliographic Instruction Program in Music." College & Research Libraries 40 (May 1979): 226-33.

A298. Jewell, T. D. "Student Reactions to a Self-Paced Library Skills Workbook Program: survey evidence." College & Research Libraries 43 (September 1982): 371-8.

A299. Johnson, Eric W. "Library Instruction for Faculty Members." Reference Librarian 10 (Spring-Summer 1984): 199-204.

A300. Johnson, Herbert Webster; Faria, Anthony J.; and Maier, Ernest L. How to Use the Business Library: with sources of business information. 5th ed. Cincinnati: South-Western, 1984.

A301. Johnson, K. A. and Plake, B. S. "Evaluation of PLATO Library Instructional Lessons: another view." Journal of Academic Librarianship 6 (July 1980): 154-8.

A302. Jolly, C. "Teaching Information-use to Science Students." Library Association Record 77 (February): 41.

A303. Jonas, E. S. "Preparation of a Slide/Tape Program for Biological Abstracts: Harvard University." Science & Technology Libraries 5 (Fall 1984): 63-7.

A304. Joseph, Margaret A., and Schmelzle, Joan C. Library Instruction Workbook: a basic introduction to the use of the UTSA Library. San Antonio, Tex.: University of Texas at San Antonio, 1976.

A305. Joyce, B. A. "Library Instruction." Oklahoma Librarian 26 (July 1976): 21-3.

A306. Karuth, L. and Clymer, E. W. "NTID Student Guide to Wallace Memorial Library. NY.: Rochester Institute of Technology, National Technology Institute for the Deaf, 1983.

A307. Katz, William Armstrong. Your Library: a reference guide. 2nd ed. New York: Holt, Rinehart & Winston, 1984.

A308. Kazemek, F. E. "Library Handbooks and Orientation in Illinois Community College Libraries." Illinois Libraries 57 (May 1975): 354-5.

A309. Keever, E. H. and Raymond, J. C. "Integrated Library Instruction on the University Campus: experiment at the University of Alabama." Journal of Academic Librarianship 2 (September 1976): 185-7.

A310. Kelley, S. J. Point-of-use Instruction in the Identification, Location, and Use of Abstracts and Indexes in Academic Libraries. Chicago: University of Chicago, 1980.

A311. Kendrick, A. W. "BI for Business Students." College & Research Libraries News No. 9 (October 1985): 482-3.

A312. Kennedy, James R. Jr. Library Research Guide to Education: illustrated search strategy and sources. ("Library Research Guides" Series, no. 3). Ann Arbor, MI.: Pierian, 1979.

A313. Kenney, D. J. "Publishing BI Articles in Discipline Journals: Social Sciences." Research Strategies 2 (Summer 1984): 128-135.

A314. Kenney, D. J. "Role of Technical Services Librarians in Library Instruction." Southeastern Librarian 31 (Spring 1981): 11-3.

A315. Kenney, D. J. "Where There Is No Vision [response to the Think tank recommendations on bibliographic instruction]." Journal of Academic Librarianship 9 (March 1983): 7-8.

A316. Kenney, P. A. and McArthur, J. N. "Designing and Evaluating a Programmed Library Instruction Text." College & Research Libraries 45 (January 1984): 35-42.

A317. Kerka, S. and Others. "LIP Service: the undergraduate library instruction program at the Ohio State University." Journal of Academic Librarianship 7 (November 1981): 279-82.

A318. Key, J. and Tollman, T. A. "Videotape as an Aid to Bibliographic Instruction." Nebraska Library Association Quarterly 12 (Fall 1981): 35-7.

A319. King, D. N. "Beyond Bibliographic Instruction." Medical Reference Services Quarterly (Summer 1984): 75-80.

A320. King, D. N. and Ory, J. C. "Effects of Library Instruction on Student Research: a case study." College & Research Libraries 42 (January 1981): 31-41.

A321. Kinney, L. C. "Librarians As Educators." Community & Junior College Journal 47 (May 1977): 10-1.

A322. Kirk, Thomas. "Concluding Comments." New Directions for Teaching and Learning (Increasing the Teaching Role of Academic Libraries) 18 (June 1984): 95-7.

A323. Kirk, Thomas. "Library Administrators and Instruction Librarians: improving relations." Journal of Academic Librarianship 6 (January 1981): 345.

A324. Kirk, Thomas. Library Research Guide to Biology: illustrated search strategy and sources. ("Library Research Guides" Series, no. 2). Ann Arbor, Michigan: Pierian, 1978.

A325. Kirk, Thomas, and Freudenthal, Juan. Annotated Bibliography on Bibliographic Instruction for Undergraduate Students. Chicago: American Library Association, 1976.

A326. Kirk, Thomas and Others. "Structuring Services and Facilities for Library Instruction." Library Trends 29 (Summer 1980): 39-53.

A327. Kirkendall, Carolyn A., ed. "Accommodating International Users: how much is too much?" Research Strategies 2 (Spring 1984): 85-7.

A328. Kirkendall, Carolyn A. "BI Liaison Project Update." College & Research Libraries News 9 (October 1984): 481-3.

A329. Kirkendall, Carolyn A. Bibliographic Instruction and the Learning Process: theory, style and motivation. (Library Orientation Series: no. 14). Ann Arbor,MI.: Pierian, 1984.

A330. Kirkendall, Carolyn A. ed. Directions for the Decade: library instruction in the 1980s. Papers presented at the Tenth Annual Conference on Library Orientation for Academic Libraries held at Eastern Michigan University, May 8-9, 1980. (Library Orientation Series, no. 12). Published for the Center of Educational Resources, Eastern Michigan University. Ann Arbor, Michigan: Pierian, 1981.

A331. Kirkendall, Carolyn A. ed. "Do Faculty Members Have Fragile Egos?" Research Strategies 2 (Winter 1984): 47-9.

A332. Kirkendall, Carolyn A. ed. "Encouraging Competence in Library Research." Research Strategies 2 (Summer 1984): 143-6.

A333. Kirkendall, Carolyn A. "Frustrations of the Bibliographic Instructor." Research Strategies 2 (Fall 1984): 188-90.

A334. Kirkendall, Carolyn A. ed. Improving Library Instruction: how to teach and how to evaluate. Papers presented at the Eighth Annual Conference on Library Orientation for Academic Libraries, Eastern Michigan University, May, 1978. (Library Orientation Series: no. 9). Published for the Center of Educational Resources, Eastern Michigan University. Ann Arbor, MI.: Pierian, 1979.

A335. Kirkendall, Carolyn A. "Improving Teaching: how a clearinghouse helps." New Directions for Teaching and Learning (Increasing the Teaching Role of Academic Libraries) 18 (June 1984): 79-84.

A336. Kirkendall, Carolyn A. ed. "Library Instruction: a column of opinion: do you consider the use of audiovisual presentations as indispensable to a successful orientation/instruction program?" Journal of Academic Librarianship 2 (January 1977): 304-5.

A337. Kirkendall, Carolyn A. "Publicizing BI." College & Research Libraries News no. 1 (January 1983): 1+.

A338. Kirkendall, Carolyn A. ed. Putting Library Instruction in Its Place: in the library and in the library school. Papers presented at the Seventh Annual Conference on Library Orientation for Academic Libraries, Eastern Michigan University, May 12-13, 1977. (Library Orientation Series: no. 8). Published for the Center of Educational Resources, Eastern Michigan University. Ann Arbor, MI.: Pierian, 1978.

A339. Kirkendall, Carolyn A. ed. Reformed Renewal in Higher Education: implications for library instruction. Papers presented at the Ninth Annual Conference on Library Orientation for Academic Libraries, Eastern Michigan University, May, 1979. (Library Orientation Series, no. 10). Published for the Center of

Educational Resources, Eastern Michigan University. Ann Arbor, MI.: Pierian, 1978.

A340. Kirkendall, Carolyn A. ed. Teaching Library Use Competence: bridging the gap from high school to college. Paper presented at the Eleventh Annual Library Instruction Conference held at Eastern Michigan University, May 7-8, 1981. (Library Orientation Series: no. 13). Published for the Center of Educational Resources, Eastern Michigan University. Ann Arbor, MI.: Pierian, 1982.

A341. Kirkendall, Carolyn A. "To Teach Manual or Online Searching?" Research Strategies 3 (Spring 1985): 93-5.

A342. Kitchens, P. H. "Engineers Meet the Library." Journal of Academic Librarianship 5 (November 1979): 277-82.

A343. Kitchens, P. H. "Library-use Instruction for Engineers at the University of Alabama." Alabama Librarian 29 (November 1977): 14-5.

A344. Kline, Laura S. and Rod, Catherine M. "Library Orientation Programs for Foreign Students: a survey." RQ 24 (Winter 1984): 210-6.

A345. Knapp, S. D. "Instructing Library Patrons About Online Reference Service." Bookmark 38 (Fall 1979): 237-42.

A346. Knight, Hattie M. The 1-2-3 Guide to Libraries. 5th ed. Dubuque, Iowa: Brown, 1976.

A347. Koolowyn, A. C. and Corby, K. "Citation: a library instruction computer game." RQ 22 (Winter 1982): 171-4.

A348. Koh, L. "Library Services to Students at the Southeast Asia Union College." Singapore Libraries 8 (1978): 22-3.

A349. Koppelman, C. "Orientation and Instruction in Academic Art Libraries." Special Libraries 67 (May-June 1976): 256-60

A350. Koren, S. "Some Thoughts on Bibliographical Instruction." NYLA Bulletin 23 (October 1975): 1+.

A351. Koren, S. "Student Library Internship Program:

Manhattanville's approach to bibliographic instruction." Bookmark 38 (Fall 1979): 243-8.

A352. Kostrewski, B. Education in Medical Information in West Germany: final report; report to the British Library R & D Department on project numbers Sl/V/047. London: City University, Centre for Information Science, 1980.

A353. Krier, M. "Bibliographic Instruction: a checklist of the literature, 1931-1975." Reference Services Review 4 (January 1976): 7-12.

A354. Krzyminski, C. "Library Instruction in a Nontraditional Setting." Wisconsin Library Bulletin 78 (Fall 1983): 113-4.

A355. Lacks, B. K. "Reference and Information Services in the Vassar College Library." Bookmark 41 (Winter 1983): 75-9.

A356. "Langara Library Overhauls Orientation Program." BCLA Reporter 21 (September-October 1977): 7-8.

A357. Langer, Monika. "Academic Libraries: fetishism of information or centre of education." Canadian Library Journal 38 (February 1981): 25-8.

A358. "Large-Scale Bibliographic Instruction -- the Illinois Experience." Research Strategies 2 (Winter 1984): 4-44.

A359. Larson, Mary Ellen and Freivalds, Dace. Pennsylvania State University Libraries. A final Report from the Public Services Research Projects. The Effect of an Instruction Program on Online Catalog Users. One of a Series of Self-Studies and Research Projects. Washington, D. C.: Association of Research Libraries, Office of Management Studies, 1985. (ERIC Document Reproduction Service No. ED 255223).

A360. LaRue, J. and Holland, J. B. "Biblioprotocol: with a brief glossary of terms often needed in Austrian and German music libraries." Notes 42 (September 1985): 29-35.

A361. Lenski, S. "Library Orientation - a way of hope for users and staff." Illinois Libraries 59 (April 1977) 293-5.

A362. Levine, R. "Bibliographic Instruction and the Community and Junior College Sections; Learning theory in action: applications in bibliographic instruction." Library of Congress Information Bulletin 39 (September 26, 1980): 381-2.

A363. Library Instruction. SPEC Kit 17. Washington, D.C.: Association of Research Libraries, Office of Management Studies, 1977. (ERIC Document Reproduction Service No. ED 251076).

A364. "Library Instruction - the right time and place." Journal of Academic Librarianship 4 (May 1978): 92-3.

A365. Library Instruction Workbook: a basic introduction to the use of the UTSA Library. San Antonio, Tex.: The University of Texas at San Antonio Library, 1978.

A366. "Library Orientation and User Instruction." Alabama Librarian 26 (September 1975): 8.

A367. "Library Orientation-Instruction Exchange (LOEX) at Eastern Michigan University Will Expand Its Services Under Terms of a Three-Year Grant of $42,771 from the Council on Library Resources." College & Research Libraries News" 8 (March 1975): 77-8.

A368. "Library Orientation-Instruction Exchange (LOEX) Expands Services." Information: News and Sources 7 (July 1975): 168.

A369. "Library Orientation-Instruction Exchange Receives CLR Grant." Law Library Journal 68 (May 1975): 178.

A370. "Library Use Instruction in Academic and Research Libraries." ARL Management Supplement 5 (September 1977): 1-6.

A371. Lindgren, J. "Toward Library Literacy." RQ 20 (Spring 1981): 233-5.

A372. Loftin, J. E. "Library Orientation and Library Instruction for Medical Students." Medical Library Association Bulletin 71 (April 1983): 207-9.

A373. Lolley, J. L. "Educating the Library User; the evolution of an individualized library instructional program at Tarrant County Junior College." Texas Library Journal 51 (Spring 1975): 30-2.

A374. Lolley, J. L. "Faculty Attitudes Toward Library Instruction; the real key to success." Oklahoma Librarian 32 (November/December 1982): 7-8.

A375. Lopez, M. D. "Chinese Spoken Here: foreign language library orientation tours." College & Research Libraries News 8 (September 1983): 265.

A376. Loughead, L. and Weston, N. "Bibliographic Instruction: extending library services to a field-based program." College & Research Libraries News No. 7 (July 1982): 235-7.

A377. Love, B. "Coping With Stress: the 14th annual workshop on instruction in library use." College & Research Libraries News 8 (September 1984): 407-8.

A378. Lubans, John. "Educating the Library User in England." MPLA Newsletter 20(5) (1975-76): 3.

A379. Lubans, John. "In Pursuit of the Educated Library User: a dilemma." Ohio Association of School Librarians Bulletin 28 (October 1976): 7-9.

A380. Lubans, John. "Library Literacy: let George do it." RQ 20 (Winter 1980): 121-3.

A381. Lubans, John. "Library Literacy [University of Colorado Experiment]." RQ 19 (Summer 1980): 325-8.

A382. Lubans, John. "Organizational Change: a public services application." Reference Librarian 10 (Spring-Summer 1984): 15-25.

A383. Lynch, M. D. "U. S. by Bus; or, What is Going On in B.I. Land?" Catholic Library World 49 (October 1977): 136-7, (November 1977): 184-6, (December 1977): 225-6, (February 1978): 309-10, (March 1978): 348-9, (April 1978): 400-1, (May 1978): 451-2.

A384. Maat, L. "On-Line Searching in a Chemistry Curriculum." IATUL Proceedings 17 (1985): 129-34.

A385. MacAdam, Barbara. "Humor in the Classroom: implications for the bibliographic instruction librarian." College & Research Libraries 46 (July 1985): 327-33.

A386. MacGregor, J. and McInnis, R. G. "Integrating Classroom Instruction and Library Research; the

cognitive functions of bibliographic network
structures." <u>Journal of Higher Education</u> 48 (January
1977): 17-38.

A387. Machalow, Robert. <u>Computer Based Library Orientation.</u>
ERIC Document Reproduction Service, 1984. (ERIC
Document Reproduction Service No. ED 252239).

A388. Machalow, Robert. <u>The New York City Subways: the</u>
<u>first ten years. A Library Research Exercise Using a</u>
<u>Computer.</u> ERIC Document Reproduction Service, 1984.
(ERIC Document Reproduction Service No. ED 255211).

A389. Maesato, S. and Herrick, K. R. "The University of
Hawaii at Hilo Library Experience." <u>HLA Journal</u> 41
(1984): 5-14.

A390. Maina, W. "Class in Library Use for Allied Health
Personnel." <u>Medical Library Association Bulletin</u> 63
(April 1975): 226-8.

A391. Malley, Ian. <u>Catalogue of UK Audiovisual Media</u>
<u>Suitable for Use in Library Instruction Courses.</u> 2nd
ed. Leicestershire, England: Loughborough University
of Technology, 1980.

A392. Malley, Ian. "Educating the Special Library User."
<u>Aslib Proceedings</u> 30 (October-November 1978): 365-72.

A393. Malley, Ian. "Library Instruction Materials Bank."
<u>Aslib Proceedings</u> 30 (July 1978): 271-6.

A394. Malley, Ian. "Library Instruction Materials Bank."
<u>Interlending Review</u> 6 (October 1978): 125-7.

A395. Malley, Ian. "Production and Use of Audiovisual Media
for User Education in UK Academic Libraries."
<u>Audiovisual Librarian</u> 8 (Autumn 1982): 185-90.

A396. Malley, Ian. "Research Into Practice in User
Education." <u>Art Libraries Journal</u> 3 (Autumn 1978):
17-26.

A397. Manning, D. J. ed. "Report of a Committee of the
University and College Libraries Section of the
Library Association of Australia Appointed to Examine
the Requirements for Reader Education Activities in
Universities and Colleges." <u>Australian Academic and</u>
<u>Research Libraries</u> 4 (December 1973): insert.

A398. Marshall, A. P. ed. "Current Library Use Instruction."
      Library Trends (Summer 1980): 3-8.

A399. Martin, J. A.   "Bibliographic Instruction in the
      Medical Library." Tennessee Librarian (Summer 1980):
      10-2.

A400. Martin, J. A. and Others. "PLATO [Programmed Logic
      for Automated Teaching Operation] in the Library."
      Southeastern Librarian 31 (Spring 1981): 14-5.

A401. McCarthy, Constance. "The Faculty Problem." Journal of
      Academic Librarianship 11 (July 1985): 142-5.

A402. McCarthy, Constance. "Library Instruction:
      observations from the reference desk." RQ 22 (Fall
      1982): 36-41.

A403. McClintock, Marsha Hamilton , comp. and ed. Training
      Users of Online Public Access Catalogs; report of a
      conference sponsored by Trinity University and the
      Council on Library Resources, San Antonio, Texas,
      January 12-14, 1983. Washington, D. C.: Council on
      Library Resources, 1983.

A404. McDonald, D. R. and Searing, S. E. "Bibliographic
      Instruction and the Development of Online Catalogs."
      College & Research Libraries 44 (January 1983): 5-11.

A405. McMillan, Patricia and Kennedy, James R., Jr.
      Library Research Guide to Sociology: illustrated
      Search Strategy and Sources. ("Library Research
      Guides" Series, no. 5). Ann Arbor, MI.: Pierian,
      1981.

A406. McNallie, Bruce. Bibliographical Instruction: where
      it's at and where it's going. ERIC Document
      Reproduction Service, 1982. (ERIC Document
      Reproduction Service No. ED 226747).

A407. McQuistion, V. F. "The Credit Course: reaffirmation
      from two university libraries: measurement; Millikin
      University." Research Strategies 2 (Fall 1984): 166-
      71.

A408. Mellon, Constance A. "Process not Product in Course-
      Integrated Instruction: a generic model of library
      research." College & Research Libraries 45 (November
      1984): 471-8.

A409. Merriam, Joyce. Helping Students Make the Transition from High School to Academic Library: a report on a study of selected library instruction programs in Massachusetts. ERIC Document Reproduction Service, 1979. (ERIC Document Reproduction Service No. ED 176783).

A410. Messman, L. "Bibliographic Instruction Coordinator; Orientation/Instruction Round-up." South Carolina Librarian 27 (Spring 1983): 19-20.

A411. Meyer, W. "Three Phases of Bibliographic Instruction." Wisconsin Library Bulletin 75 (March 1979): 63-5.

A412. Miller, A. C. "Round Robin Library Tour." Journal of Academic Librarianship 6 (September 1980): 215-8.

A413. Miller, C. R. "Scientific Literature as Hierarchy: library instruction and Robert M. Gagne." College & Research Libraries 43 (September 1982): 385-90.

A414. Miller, M. M. "North Dakota State University Library Uses New Technology in Library Use Instruction." MPLA Newsletter 20 No. 2 (1975-76): 12.

A415. Miller, S. W. Library Use Instruction in Selected American Colleges. Chicago, Illinois: University of Chicago, 1976.

A416. Miller, Wayne Stuart. Library Use Instruction in Selected American Colleges. Urbana, Ill.: University of Illinois Graduate School of Library Science, Occasional Papers no. 134, 1978.

A417. Mills, R. K. "Legal Research Instruction After the First Year of Law School." Law Library Journal 76 (Summer 1983): 603-4.

A418. Mills, R. K. "Legal Research Instruction in Law Schools, the State-of-the-Art; or, Why Law School Graduates Do Not Know How to Find the Law." Law Library Journal 70 (August 1977): 343-8.

A419. Mitchel, M. "Library Skills Workbook at Stephens College." Show-Me Libraries 32 (January 1981): 32-3.

A420. Molendyke, Joseph A. "Assessing the Efficacy of Library Orientation in the Regional Campus System." Technological Horizons in Education 8 (March 1981): 52-3.

A421. Mood, Terry Ann. "Foreign Students and the Academic Library." RQ 22 (Winter 1982): 175-80.

A422. Morris, Jacquelyn. "BI Statistics Tips." College & Research Libraries News 2 (February 1984): 86-7.

A423. Morris, Jacquelyn. Bibliographic Instruction in Academic Libraries. A Review of the Literature and Selected Bibliography. New York: Syracuse University. ERIC Clearinghouse on Information Resources, 1979. (ERIC Document Reproduction Service No. ED 180505).

A424. Morris, Jacquelyn and Elkins, Elizabeth A. Library Searching: resources and strategies with examples from the environmental sciences. New York: Jeffrey Norton, 1978.

A425. Morse, Grant W. Concise Guide to Library Research. 2nd rev. ed. New York: Fleet Academic Editions, 1975.

A426. Morton, Leslie T. How to Use a Medical Library. 6th ed. London: Heinemann Medical, 1979.

A427. Mount, Ellis, ed. Training of Sci-Tech Librarians and Library Users. (Science and Technology Libraries Vol. 1, no. 3). New York: Haworth, 1981.

A428. Nagy, L. A. and Thomas, J. L. "Evaluation of the Teaching Effectiveness of Two Library Instructional Videotapes." College & Research Libraries 42 (January 1981): 26-30.

A429. Neelameghan, A. "Training of University Students of Engineering in the Use of Information." Library Science with a Slant to Documentation 15 (December 1978): 201-3.

A430. "New York Library Instruction Clearinghouse." Information Hotline 8 (September 1976): 10.

A431. "New York Library Instruction Clearinghouse Has been Established at the F. Franklin Moon Library, SUNY College of Environmental Science and Forestry in Syracuse, New York." College & Research Libraries News 3 (March 1976): 70.

A432. Newell, U. "User Education: are new approaches needed? An international conference held at Trinity College, Cambridge University, 5-8 September 1979." Australian Academic and Research Libraries 11 (March 1980): 56-7.

A433. Nielsen, B. "Teacher or intermediary: alternative professional models in the information age." College & Research Libaries 43 (May 1982): 183-91.

A434. Nieuwenhuysen, P. "Library User Education and Promotion of the Online Information Retrieval Service at the Vrije Universtiteit Brussel." IATUL Proceedings 17 (1985): 39-48.

A435. Oberman, Cerise and Strauch, Katina. eds. Theories of Bibliographic Education: designs for teaching New York: Bowker, 1982.

A436. Oberman, Cerise. "Patterns for Research." New Directions for Teaching and Learning (Increasing the Teaching Role of Academic Libraries) 18 (June 1984): 35-43.

A437. Oberman-Soroka, Cerise, ed. Proceedings from the Southeastern Conference on Approaches to Bibliographic Instruction, March 16-17, 1978. Charleston, SC.: Continuing Education Office, College of Charleston, 1978.

A438. Oberman-Soroka, Cerise, ed. Proceedings from the 2nd Southeastern Conference on Approaches to Bibliographic Instruction. March 22-23, 1979. Charleston, SC.: Continuing Education Office, College of Charleston, 1980.

A439. O'Connor, S. V. "Second International User Education Conference." Australian Academic and Research Libraries. 12 (December 1981): 270-1.

A440. O'Donnell, M. "Library Instruction During a Period of Retrenchment." Bookmark 38 (Fall 1979): 231-6.

A441. Olaniyan, B. F. and others. "Instructing Students in the Use of the Library in the University of Lagos." Nigerian Libraries 11 (April-August 1975): 123-33.

A442. Olevnik, Peter P. "Non-Formalized Point-of-use Library Instruction: a survey." Catholic Library World 50 (December 1978): 218-20.

A443. Olivetti, L. James. "Utilizing Natural Structure of the Research Literature in Psychology as a Model for Bibliographic Instruction." Behavioral & Social Sciences Librarian 1 (Fall 1979): 43-46.

A444. "Online Reference Services' Impact on Bibliographic Instruction." Research Strategies 3 (Winter 1985): 40-3.

A445. "Orientation Clearinghouse Set Up At SUNY-Syracuse." Library Journal 101 (March 1, 1976): 649-50.

A446. Ormondroyd, J. L. "Bibliographic Instruction in an Undergraduate Library." Catholic Library World 55 (April 1984): 395-8.

A447. Ota, Y. "Color Sign System of Hamilton Library, University of Hawaii." Graphic Design No. 75 (September 1979): 37-42.

A448. Otto, Theophil M. "The Academic Librarian of the 21st Century: public service and library education in the year 2000." Journal of Academic Librarianship 8 (May 1982): 85-8.

A449. Palmer, V. E. "BI for The Invisible University." College & Research Libraries News 1 (January 1982): 12-3.

A450. Parsch, J. "Bibliographic Instruction: a common sense approach." Arkansas Libraries 42 (June 1985): 6-10.

A451. Pask, J. M. "Bibliographic Instruction In Business Libraries." Special Libraries 72 (October 1981): 370-8.

A452. Pastine, Maureen. "Library Instruction and Reference Service: administration of a bibliographic instruction program in the academic library." Reference Librarian 10 (Spring-Summer 1984): 181-89.

A453. Paterson, E. R. "Assessment of College Student Library Skills." RQ 17 (Apring 1978): 226-9.

A454. Paterson, E. R. "How Effective Is Library Instruction?" RQ 18 (Summer 1979): 376-7.

A455. Paterson, E. R. "Just-for-fun Quizzes Encourage Student Participation in Library Instruction." The Unabashed Librarian No. 52 (1984): 3-4.

A456. Pausch, Lois M. and Koch, J. "Technical Services Librarians in Library Instruction." Libri 31 (September 1981): 198-204.

A457. Pearce, B. L. "Tuition in Library Use as a Part of Open University Preparatory Courses." Library Review 25 (Autumn 1976): 254-6.

A458. Pearson, P. and Tiefel, Virginia. "Evaluating Undergraduate Library Instruction at the Ohio State University." Journal of Academic Librarianship 7 (January 1982): 351-7.

A459. Pearson, R. C. and Frandsen, R. "Library Instruction in a Multi-Cultural Setting." Hawaii Library Association Journal 40 (1983): 33-6.

A460. Peele, David. "Librarians as Teachers: some reality, mostly myth." Journal of Academic Librarianship 10 (November 1984): 267-71.

A461. Person, R. "Long-term Evaluation of Bibliographic Instruction: lasting encouragement." College & Research Libraries 42 (January 1981): 19-25.

A462. Phadnis, S. P. and Others. "Training of Agricultural Scientists in Information Use." Library Science with a Slant to Documentation 15 (December 1978): 196-8.

A463. Phillips,L. "Making Library Instruction More Palatable." American Vocational Journal 52 (April 1977): 57-8.

A464. Phillips, L. and Raup, E. A. "Comparing Methods for Teaching Use of Periodical Indexes." Journal of Academic Librarianship 4 (January 1979): 420-3.

A465. Phillips, Linda L. "More Information: bibliographic instruction resources." New Directions for Teaching and Learning (Increasing the Teaching Role of Academic Libraries) 18 (June 1984): 85-94.

A466. Phipps, S. and Dickstein, R. "Library Skills Program at the University of Arizona: testing evaluation, and critique." Journal of Academic Librarianship 5 (September 1979): 205-14.

A467. Pickett, Nell Ann. Using the Library. (Harper Studies in Language and Literature). New York: Harper & Row, 1975.

A468. Pickert, S. M. and Chwalek, A. B. "Integrating Bibliographic Research Skills into a Graduate Program in Education." Catholic Library World 55 (April 1984); 392-4.

A469. Piele, L. J. and Yamel, B. "Reference Assistance Project at the University of Wisconsin-Parkside." College & Research Libraries News 3 (March 1982): 83-4.

A470. Pierce, B. A. "Librarians and Teachers: where is the common ground?" Catholic Library World 53 (November 1981): 164-7.

A471. Pinson, J. "Smoke Signals from Australia." Learning Today 14 (Spring 1981): 18-21.

A472. Plum, Stephen H. "Library Use and the Development of Critical Thought." New Directions for Teaching and Learning (Increasing the Teaching Role of Academic Libraries) 18 (June 1984): 25-33.

A473. Port, J. S. "Continuing Education in Information Retrieval Techniques for Clinicians." Medical Library Association Bulletin 68 (April 1980): 238-40.

A474. Poyer, R. K. "Improved Library Services Through User Education." Medical Library Association Bulletin 65 (April 1977): 296-7.

A475. Prince, William W. ed. Directory of Academic Library Instruction Programs in Virginia. Virginia: Virginia Library Association, 1977.

A476. Quiring, Virginia and Others. comps. Academic Library Instruction in Kansas. A Directory. Manhattan, Kansas: Kansas State University Library, 1980. (ERIC Document Reproduction Service No. ED 206308).

A477. Rader, Hannelore B., ed. Academic Library Instruction: objectives, programs, and faculty involvement. Papers presented at the Fourth Annual Conference on Library Orientation for Academic Libraries, Eastern Michigan University, May 9-11, 1974. (Library Orientation Series: no. 5). Published for the Center of Educational Resources, Eastern Michigan University. Ann Arbor, Mich.: Pierian, 1975.

A478. Rader, Hannelore B. An Assessment of Ten Academic Library Instruction Programs in the United States and

Canada. A council on Library Resources Fellowship Report, Eastern Michigan University, Ypsilanti, 1976. (Photocopied.)

A479. Rader, Hannelore B. "Bibliographic Instruction." Reference Services Review 10 (Spring 1982): 65-6.

A480. Rader, Hannelore B. "Bibliographic Instruction." Reference Services Review 10 (Fall 1982): 89-90.

A481. Rader, Hannelore B. "Bibliographic Instruction: is it a discipline?" Reference Services Review 10 (Winter 1982): 75-6.

A482. Rader, Hannelore B. "Bibliographic Instruction Programs in Academic Libraries." New Directions for Teaching and Learning (Increasing the Teaching Role of Academic Libraries) 18 (June 1984): 63-78.

A483. Rader, Hannelore B., ed. Faculty Involvement in Library Instruction. Papers presented at the Fifth Annual Conference on Library Orientation for Academic Libraries, Eastern Michigan University, May 15-17, 1975. (Library Orientation Series: no. 6). Published for the Center of Educational Resources, Eastern Michigan University. Ann Arbor, MI.: Pierian, 1976.

A484. Rader, Hannelore B. A Guide to Academic Library Instruction. (Foundations in Library and Information Science Series: vol. 7). Greenwich, Conn.: JAI Press, 1979.

A485. Rader, Hannelore B. ed. Library Instruction in the Seventies: state of the art. Papers presented at the Sixth Annual Conference on Library Orientation for Academic Libraries, Eastern Michigan University, May 13-14, 1976. (Library Orientation Series: no. 7). Published for the Center of Educational Resources, Eastern Michigan University. Ann Arbor, MI.: Pierian, 1977.

A486. Rader, Hannelore B. "Library Orientation and Instruction -- 1982." Reference Services Review 11 (Summer 1983): 57-65.

A487. Rader, Hannelore B. "Second International Conference on User Education." College & Research Libraries News No. 10 (November 1981): 359.

A488. Radford, N. A. "Why Bother With Reader Education?" New Zealand Libraries 43 (December 1980): 53-6.

A489. Rajagopalan, T. S. and Rajan, T. N. "Use of Information in Science and Research with Emphasis on National Development: some Indian experiences." International Forum on Information and Documentation 9 (July 1984): 3-9.

A490. Ramey, M. A. "Learning to Think About Libraries: focusing on attitudinal change for remedial studies students." Research Strategies 3 (Summer 1985): 125-30.

A491. Ramey, M. A. and Spanjer, A. "Videotaping Bibliographic Instruction: a confrontation with self." Research Strategies 2 (Spring 1984): 71-5.

A492. "Reader Education, Two Comments." Australian Academic and Research Libraries 6(June 1975): 92-5.

A493. Ready, S. K. "Putting the Online Catalog in Its Place." Research Strategies 2 (Summer 1984): 119-27.

A494. Ready, S. K. and Saltzman, L. E. "Collaboration on Integrated Library Instruction: a reaction." Research Strategies 2 (Spring 1984): 76-81.

A495. Reid, B. J. "Aston Intro-Active: a library game for new undergraduates." Research Strategies 2 (Summer 1984): 108-18.

A496. Renford, Beverly. "Self-paced Workbook Program for Beginning College Students." Journal of Academic Librarianship 4 (September 1978): 200-3.

A497. Renford, Beverly and Hendrickson, Linnea. Bibliographic Instruction: a handbook. New York: Neal-Schuman, 1980.

A498. Renwick, K. D. "Production or Protraction?" Audiovisual Librarian 4 (Autumn 1977): 23-4.

A499. Reusch, R. "The Search for Analogous Legal Authority: how to find it when you don't know what you're looking for." Legal Reference Services Quarterly 4 (Fall 1984): 33-8.

A500. Rice, James, Jr. Teaching Library Use: a guide for library instruction. (Contributions in Librarianship and Information Service Series: no. 37). Westport, Conn.: Greenwood, 1981.

A501. Richardson, L. L. "Teaching Basic Skills: past tense, future perfect." Reference Services Review 12 (Spring 1984): 67-76.

A502. Ridgeway, P. M. "Orientation/Instruction Round-Up." South Colorado Librarian 23 (Spring 1979): 6-7, (Fall 1979): 17-9.

A503. Ridgeway, P. M. "Taught How to Teach? Instruction Round-Up." South Colorado Librarian 24 (Fall 1980): 24.

A504. Ridgeway, Trish. Library Orientation Methods, Mental Maps, and Public Services Planning. ERIC Document Reproduction Service, 1983. (ERIC Document Reproduction Service No. ED 247942).

A505. Roberts, Anne. "The Changing Role of the Academic Instruction Librarian." Catholic Library World 51 (Feburary 1980): 283-5.

A506. Roberts, Anne. Library Instruction for Librarians. (Library Science Text Series). Littleton, Colo.: Libraries Unlimited, 1982.

A507. Roberts, Anne. Organizing and Managing a Library Instruction Program. Checklists. Chicago: American Library Association, Association of College and Research Libraries, 1979. (ERIC Document Reproduction Service No. ED 176731).

A508. Rodda, R. R. "Questions Most Often Asked in Our Science Library." Unabashed Librarian No. 23 (1977): 22.

A509. Rudnik, Mary Chrysantha. "Bibliographic Instruction: make it more than bibliographic first aid." Catholic Library World 55 (April 1984): 388-91.

A510. Sadow, S. and Beede, B. R. "Library Instruction in American Law Schools." Law Library Journal 68 (February 1975): 27-32.

A511. Sayles, Jeremy W. "Course Information Analysis: foundation for creative library support." Journal of Academic Librarianship 10 (January 1985): 343-5.

A512. Sayles, Jeremy W. "Opinion About Library Instruction." Southeastern Librarian 30 (Winter 1980): 198-200.

A513. Schechter, I. R. Library Research Guide for Art History Graduate Students. East Lansing, Michigan: Michigan State University, Department of Art, 1978.

A514. Schirmer, R. and Newman, G. C. "Bibliographic Instruction: library and information retrieval instruction; competency testing." College & Research Libraries News 8 (September 1982): 259.

A515. Schlicke, P. A. "The Use of the Computer in a Course of Instruction for Physical Sciences Students." IATUL Proceedings 17 (1985): 145-50.

A516. Schmidmaier, D. "New University Library Buildings and Library Instruction." IATUL Proceedings 8 (1976): 29-36.

A517. Schobert, T. "Bibliographic Instruction: Exploring the New Technology for Library Instruction." College & Research Libraries News 9 (October 1983): 337.

A518. Schobert, T. "Term-paper Counseling: individualized bibliographic instruction." RQ 22 (Winter 1982): 146-51.

A519. Schramm, J. V. and Stewart, F. H. "Search for Chief Joseph; a single-subject approach to library orientation and instruction." West Virginia Libraries 32 (Summer 1979): 17-22.

A520. Schryer, A. "Library Orientation at Statistics Canada Library." Feliciter 21 (September 1975): 6-7.

A521. Schwartz, Barbara A., and Bruton, Susan. Teaching Library Skills in Freshman English: an undergraduate library's experience. (Contributions to Librarianship Series: no. 6). Austin, Tex.: University of Texas at Austin. General Libraries, 1981.

A522. Schwartz, D. G. "Bibliographic Instruction: a public relations perspective." Medical Reference Services Quarterly 3 (Summer 1984): 43-9.

A523. Schwarz, P. J. "Learning to Use Microform Equipment: a self-instructional approach." Microform Review 4 (October 1975): 262-5.

A524. Schwob, E. "Orientation: library program shows gratifying results." Feliciter 23 (Feburary 1977): 3.

A525. Selegean, J. C. et al. "Long-Range Effectiveness of Library Use Instruction." College & Research Libraries 44 (November 1983): 476-80.

A526. Serving Deaf Students in Academic Libraries. ERIC Document Reproduction Service, 1983. (ERIC Document Reproduction Service No. ED 235829).

A527. Sharma, R. N. "Bibliographic Instruction: have we succeeded?" Library Scene 7 (June 1978): 33-4.

A528. Shelden, P. R. Effect of Orientation and Instruction on Use Of, and Satisfaction With, a Government Documents Collection in a University Library. Ann Arbor, Michigan: University of Michigan, 1982.

A529. Sheppard, M. O. "Information Seeking by TAFE Trade Student Teachers." Australian Academic and Research Libraries 14 (September 1983): 149-57.

A530. Shrigley, R. M. "Reader Education." New Library World 82 (March 1981): 42-3.

A531. Silvernail, P. W. "Library Instruction Materials in CUNY: a review." LACUNY Journal 4 (Fall 1975): 37-40.

A532. Simon, Rose Ann. "The Faculty/Librarian Partnership." New Directions for Teaching and Learning (Increasing the Teaching Role of Academic Libraries) 18 (June 1984): 55-61.

A533. Simpson, Antony E. Guide to Library Research in Public Adlministration. New York: Center for Productive Public Management, John Jay College of Criminal Justice, 1976.

A534. Skinner, Jane and Violette, Judith. Comps. A Directory of Library Instruction Programs in Indiana Academic Libraries. Indiana: Indiana Library Association, 1980. (ERIC Document Reproduction Service No. ED 191487).

A535. Smalley, T. N. "Bibliographic Instruction in Academic Libraries: questioning some assumptions." Journal of Academic Librarianship 3 (November 1977)1: 280-3.

A536. Smith, Barbara J. "Background Characteristics and Education Needs of a Group of Instruction Librarians in Pennsylvania." College & Research Libraries 43 (May 1982): 199-207.

A537. Smith, Dana E. and Hutton, Steve M. "Back at 8:00 AM -- Microcomputer Library Reference Support Programs." Collegiate Microcomputer 2 (November 1984): 289-94.

A538. Smith, G. M. "Cause for Concern." New Library World 78 (October 1977): 189-90.

A539. Smith, G. M. "Library-based Information Services in Higher Education: towards a reappraisal." Aslib Proceedings 27 (June 1975): 239-46.

A540. Smith, J. M. and Winkworth, F. V. Library User Education; a bibliography of teaching materials for schools and colleges of further education. England: British Library Research & Development Department, 1978.

A541. Smith, P. B. "The HELP! Session as Bibliographic Instruction." Unabashed Librarian No. 51 (1984): 23-24.

A542. Smith, S. A. "Bibliographic Instruction: a selfish view." Georgia Librarian 19: (Feburary 1982): 12.

A543. Snyder, S. "Library Instruction: learning how." Cornell University Library Bulletin No. 204 (April 1977): 7.

A544. "Southeastern Bibliographic Instruction Clearinghouse." Information Hotline 9 (November 1977): 5.

A545. Spencer, K. L. "Legal Research in a Slide Carousel." Law Library Journal 71 (February 1978): 156-7.

A546. Stamps, Margaret, and Phelps, Eloise. Library Roundup Program for Learning Library Skills. Pueblo: University of Southern Colorado, 1975.

A547. Stebelman, S. "Self-Paced Tours at UN-L [University of Nebraska, Lincoln]." Nebraska Library Association Quarterly 9 (Winter 1978): 23-5.

A548. Steidinger, Jana Reeg and Trzebiatowski, Elaine. Library Study Guide for Business. ERIC Document Reproduction Service, 1984. (ERIC Document Reproduction Service No. ED 255217).

A549. Sternberg, M. "There Are No Stupid Questions: a

university library film." Unabashed Librarian No. 18 (Winter 1976): 27-8.

A550. Stevenson, Malcolm B. "Education in the Use of Information in University and Academic Environment." Aslib Proceedings 28 (January 1976): 17-21.

A551. Stevenson, Malcolm B. "Education of Users of Libraries and Information Services." Journal of Documentation 33 (March 1977): 243-4.

A552. Stevenson, Malcolm B. User Education Programmes: a study of their development, organization, methods and assessments. London: British Library, 1977.

A553. Stockard, Joan. comp. A Directory of Bibliographic Instruction Programs in New England Academic Libraries. Massachusetts: Association of College and Research Libraries. New England Chapter, 1978. (ERIC Document Reproduction Service No. ED 171259).

A554. Stoffle, Carla J. and Larson, J. "Academic Library Skills; how do Wisconsin academic libraries teach library use?" Wisconsin Library Bulletin 73 (July 1977): 159-60.

A555. Stoffle, Carla J. and Others. "Teaching, Research, and Service: the academic library's role." New Directions for Teaching and Learning (Increasing the Teaching Role of Academic Libraries) 18 (June 1984): 3-14.

A556. Sturges, R. P. "Subject Bibliography in the Service of History." Library Review 26 (Summer 1978): 90-4.

A557. Sugranes, M. R. and Neal, J. A. "Evaluation of a Self-Paced Bibliographic Instruction Course." College & Research Libraries 44 (November 1983): 444-457.

A558. Sullivan, C. "Survey of In-House User Education in Special Libraries." Aslib Proceedings. 31 (July 1979): 322-3.

A559. Surprenant, T. T. Comparison of Lecture and Programmed Instruction in the Teaching of Basic Catalog Card and Bibliographic Index Information. Madison, Wisconsin: University of Wisconsin, 1979.

A560. Surprenant, T. T. "Learning Theory, Lecture, and Programmed Instruction Text: an experiment in

bibliographic instruction." <u>College & Research</u>
<u>Libraries</u> 43 (January 1982): 31-7.

A561. Tanzer, T. J. "Training Engineering Students to Use
the Library." <u>IATUL Proceedings</u> 9 (1977): 59-65.

A562. Taylor, D. "Library Orientation for Health Sciences
Center Secretaries." <u>Medical Library Association</u>
<u>Bulletin</u> 70 (October 1982): 411-2.

A563. Taylor, J. H. "Research Resources for the College."
<u>Improving College & University Teaching</u> 26 (Winter
1978): 89-90.

A564. "Teaching Library at Sangamon State University."
<u>Journal of Academic Librarianship</u> 1 (September 1975):
28-9.

A565. Ternberg, M. G.   "BI for Accounting Students."
<u>College & Research Libraries News</u> No. 6 (June 1985):
293-4.

A566. Ternberg, M. G. "Library Orientation for Business
Students: a case study." <u>College & Research Library</u>
<u>News</u> no. 4 (April 1983): 114-5.

A567. "These Students Need to Know This!" <u>Learning Today</u> 13
Summer 1980): 24-9.

A568. Thesing, Jane I. "Marketing Academic Library
Bibliographic Instruction Programs: case and
commentary." <u>Research Strategies</u> 3 (Winter 1985): 29-
36.

A569. Thomas, Joy and Ensor, Pat. "University Faculty and
Library Instruction." <u>RQ</u> 23 (Summer 1984): 431-7.

A570. Thompson, G. J. "Computer Use in LMED 100, How to Use
the Library." <u>College & Research Libraries News</u> 2
(February 1984): 83.

A571. Thompson, G. J. and Stevens, B. R. "Library Science
Students Develop Pathfinders." <u>College & Research</u>
<u>Libraries News</u> No. 5 (May 1985): 224-5.

A572. Thomson, M. and Wilkinson, E. H. "Learning to Use a
University Library Subject Catalogue." <u>Australian</u>
<u>Academic and Research Libraries</u> 9 (June 1978): 71-80.

A573. Tiefel, Virginia. <u>The Ohio State University UVC 100</u>

Library Instruction Program. Columbus, Ohio: Ohio State University, 1979. (ERIC Document Reproduction Service No. ED 191482).

A574. Tiefel, Virginia and Shaw, J. "Freshman Library Instruction at Hiram College; a decade of progress." Ohio Library Associationn Bulletin 52 (April 1982): 25-8.

A575. Tierney, Judith. Basic Library Skills: a self-paced workbook. ERIC Document Reproduction Service, 1984. (ERIC Document Reproduction Service No. ED 247941).

A576. Tierno, M. J. and Lee J. H. "Developing and Evaluating Library Research Skills in education: a model for course-integrated bibliographic instruction." RQ 22 (Spring 1983): 284-91.

A577. Tietjen, M. C. "Library Instruction Improvement Association." Library Scene 4 (June 1975): 12-3.

A578. Tiffany, C. J. and Wieners, S. "Pretty Packages Aid Learning: Stout has many self-paced library instruction formats." Wisconsin Library Bulletin 72 (May 1976): 127-8.

A579. Ting, R. N. H. "Library Workshops for Engineers: the Buffalo Experiment." Special Libraries 66 (March 1975): 140-2.

A580. Tippet, H. "Evaluating the Lawrence University Program." Wisconsin Library Bulletin 75 (March 1979): 62.

A581. Tobin, C. M. "Online Computer Bibliographic Searching as an Instructional Tool." Reference Services Review 12 (Winter 1984): 71-3.

A582. Todd, Alden. Finding Facts Fast. 2nd ed. Berkeley, CA.: Speed Press, 1979.

A583. "Too Bad About That Extra Effort." Learning Today 12 (Winter 1979): 35.

A584. Toomer, C. "Bibliographic Instruction in Historically Black Colleges and Universities in North Carolina." North Carolina Libraries 41 (Spring 1983): 28-31.

A585. Tucker, John Mark. Articles on Library Instruction in Colleges and Universities, 1876-1932. Urbana, Ill.:

University of Illinois, Graduate School of Library Science, 1980.

A586. Tucker, John Mark. "Emerson's Library Legacy: concepts of bibliographic instruction." New Directions for Teaching and Learning (Increasing the Teaching Role of Academic Libraries) 18 (June 1984): 15-24.

A587. Tucker, John Mark. "Experiment in Bibliographic Instruction at Wabash College." College & Research Libraries 38 (May 1977): 203-9.

A588. Tucker, John Mark. "User Education in Academic Libraries: a century in retrospect." Library Trends 29 (Summer 1980): 9-27.

A589. "Two Approaches to Instruction of Library Patrons in Research Materials." MPLA Newsletter 20(2) (1975-76): 12.

A590. "U. Cal/Berkeley Downgrades Respected Bib I Course." American Libraries 16 (June 1985): 370.

A591. "UM [University of Mississippi] Library Initiates Outreach Programs." Mississippi Library News 41 (December 1977): 208.

A592. "University of Delaware Uses PLATO for Bibliographic Instruction." Library Journal 106 (June 15, 1981): 1266.

A593. "Unmanned Information Relieves Staff [at Bradford University]." Library Associationn Record 81 (Feburary 1979): 59.

A594. Urbanek, V. "INFORM: library information at your fingertips." Information Technology and Libraries 1 (December 1982): 336-41.

A595. User Instructions for Online Catalogs in ARL Libraries. Kit 93. Washington, D. C.: Association of Research Libraries, Office of Management Studies, 1983.

A596. "UT-Austin Library Teaches Engineering Students." Library Journal 110 (September 1, 1985): 120.

A597. VanderMeer, P. F. "Choosing Your Media for Library Instruction." Media Spectrum 9(1) (1982): 16-8.

A598. Van Pulis, Noelle. <u>User and Staff Education for the Online Catalog.</u> Paper presented at the Spring meeting of the Northern Ohio Technical Services Librarians (University Heights, Ohio, June 8, 1985). ERIC Document Reproduction Service, 1985. (ERIC Document Reproduction Service No. ED 257478).

A599. Van Pulis, Noelle. "User Education for an Online Catalog: a workshop approach." <u>RQ</u> 21 (Fall 1981): 61-9.

A600. Vasudeva Rao, K. N. "Training of Practicing Engineers in the Information Use." <u>Library Science with a Slant to Documentation</u> 15 (December 1978): 199-200.

A601. Vernon, K. D. C. "Introducing Users to Sources of Information: the approach of the London Business School." <u>Aslib Proceedings</u> 27 (November-December 1975): 468-73.

A602. Vertrees, R. L. and Murfin, M. E. "Teaching the Legislative Process: an evaluation of classroom and library instruction and a legislative history exercise." <u>Government Publications Review</u> 7A(6) (1980): 505-15.

A603. Vezier, L. "10 Years of Turning Out Engineers for Using Scientific and Technical Information at the Compiegne University of Technology." <u>IATUL Proceedings</u> 17 (1985): 151-2.

A604. Vincent, C. P. "Bibliographic Instruction in the Humanities: the need to stress imagination." <u>Research Strategies</u> 2 (Fall 1984): 179-84.

A605. Vincent, C. P. "How about the Reader's Guide?" <u>Research Strategies</u> 3 (Spring 1985): 87-9.

A606. Voit, B. and Tribble, J. "Workbook Approach to Teaching Basic Library Skills in the Community College: two points of view." <u>Kentucky Library Association Bulletin</u> 44 (Winter 1980): 4-8.

A607. Volker, J. "AV and Reader Education; report of a seminar held at the Australian National University 30 November and 1 December 1978." <u>Australian Academic and Research Libraries</u> 10 (June 1979): 120-1.

A608. Volker, J. "Practice Makes Perfect, I Hope; Library Skills Tutorials at the ANU Library." <u>Australian</u>

Academic and Research Libraries 15 (March 1984): 16-22.

A609. Vuturo, R. A. "Beyond the Library Tour: those who can, must teach." Wilson Library Bulletin 51 (May 1977): 736-40.

A610. Vuturo, R. A. and Cowdrick, C. E. "Recycling the College Library." College Composition and Communication 28 (Feburary 1977): 57-8.

A611. Walker, L. K. "Texas Collection and the Freshman Research Paper." Texas Libraries 43 (Fall 1981): 108-12.

A612. Walser, K. P. and Kruse, K. W. "College Course for Nurses on the Utilization of Library Resources." Medical Library Association Bulletin 65 (April 1977): 265-7.

A613. Ward, J. E. "Library and Bibliographic Instruction in Southeastern Academic Libraries." Southeastern Librarian 26 (Fall 1976): 148-59.

A614. Ward, S. N. and Osegueda, L. M. "Teaching University Student End-Users About Online Searching." Science & Technology Libraries 5 (Fall 1984): 17-31.

A615. Webber, M. and McClure, Charles R. "Educating the Academic Library User: issues, sources, and comments." Oklahoma Librarian 30 (July 1980): 16-20.

A616. Weir, K. M. "Teaching Library." Special Libraries Association. Geography and Map Division Bulletin 109 (September 1977): 34-9.

A617. Welch, C. B. "User Education." Texas Library Journal 59 (Winter 1983): 118-9.

A618. Werking, Richard H. "Evaluating Bibliographic Education: a review and critique." Library Trends 29 (Summer 1980): 153-72.

A619. Werking, Richard H. "Lawrence Library Receives Grant." Wisconsin Library Bulletin 73 (March 1977): 50.

A620. Werking, Richard H. The Library and College: some programs of library instruction. ERIC Document Reproduction Service, 1976. (ERIC Document Reproduction Service No. ED 127917).

A621. Werking, Richard H. "Library Service Enhancement." Wisconsin Library Bulletin 73 (November 1977): 279.

A622. Wesley, T. L. and Werrell, E. "Making the Most of a Limited Opportunity: instruction for periodical assignments." Research Strategies 3 (Summer 1985): 108-15.

A623. Whildin, Sara L. "Library Instruction in Pennsylvania Academic Libraries: a survey summary." Pennsylvania Library Association Bulletin 31 (January 1976): 8.

A624. White, Donald J. "Orientation Course Aids Staff on the Job." Canadian Library Journal 36 (February-April 1979): 17-20.

A625. White, Donald J. "Workbooks for Basic Library Instruction." Canadian Library Journal 38 (August 1981): 213-9.

A626. Whitmore, Marilyn P. Instructing the Academic Library User: historical background and utilization of audiovisual presentations. ERIC Document Reproduction Service, 1979. (ERIC Document Reproduction Service No. ED 202458).

A627. Whitmore, Marilyn P. Instructing the Academic Library User in the United States and Britain: a review of the literature and the state-of-the-art in Oxford. ERIC Document Reproduction Service, 1981. (ERIC Document Reproduction Service No. ED 207599).

A628. Wilkinson, E. H.; and others. The Use of a University Library's Subject Catalogue: report of a research project. North Ryde, New South Wales: Macquarie University, 1977.

A629. Williams, Dudley A. Annotated Bibliography for Organizational Communication, 1960-1976. Special Report Number 38. Athens, Ohio: Ohio University, College of Communication, 1980. (ERIC Document Reproduction Service No. ED 195250).

A630. Williams, E. "Introduction to Science Literature: a library assignment for general biology students." Research Strategies 2 (Spring 1984): 65-70.

A631. Williams, M. and Davis, Elisabeth B. "Evaluation of PLATO [Programmed Logic for Automatic Teaching Operation] Library Instructional Lessons." Journal of Academic Librarianship 5 (March 1979): 14-19.

A632. Williams, Nyal Z., and Tsukamoto, Jack T. eds.
       Library Instruction and Faculty Development: growth
       opportunities in the academic community. Paper
       presented at the Twenty-Third Midwest Academic
       Librarian's Conference held at Ball State University,
       May, 1978. (Library Orientation Series: no. 11). Ann
       Arbor, Mich.: Pierian, 1980.

A633. Wilson, J. H. "Librarians: introverted or integrated."
       Australian Academic and Research Libraries 8 (June
       1977): 87-93.

A634. Wilson, Lizabeeth A. The Connection Between Library
       Skills Instruction and the Developmental Writer:
       administrative implications. Paper presented at the
       Annual meeting of the Conference on College
       Composition (36th, Minneapolis, Minnesota, March 22,
       1985). ERIC Document Reproduction Service, 1985. (ERIC
       Document Reproduction Service No. ED 256372).

A635. Wolf, Carolyn E. and Wolf, Richard. Basic Library
       Skills: a short course. Jefferson, NC.: McFarland,
       1981. Second edition, 1986.

A636. Wolman, Yecheskel. Chemical Information: a practical
       guide to utilization. (A Wiley-Interscience
       Publication). New York: John Wiley & Sons, 1983.

A637. "Wood [Junior College] Exhibits [library orientation
       materials] at SELA. Mississippi Library News 40
       (December 1976): 228.

A638. Wood, K. "Viewpoint: how exactly does one interpret
       the term user education?" Art Libraries Journal 3
       (Autumn 1978): 2-4.

A639. Wood, Richard J. A One Credit, Self-Paced Library
       Research Course and Its Impact on the Knowledge and
       Attitude Base of Slippery Rock University Students.
       ERIC Document Reproduction Service, 1983. (ERIC
       Document Reproduction Service No. ED 241026).

A640. Wood, Richard J. "Impact of a Library Research Course
       on Students at Slippery Rock University." Journal of
       Librarianship 10 (November 1984): 278-84.

A641. Wood, Richard J. Vacation College: an opportunity for
       librarians. ERIC Document Reproduction Service, 1979.
       (ERIC Document Reproduction Service No. ED 181913).

A642. Woolpy, J. H. "Information Retrieval for Introductory Science Courses." American Biology Teacher 29 (March 1977): 162-4.

A643. Woolsey, B.; and others. "Academic-Year Openers: three ideas from the field." American Libraries 15 (September 1984): 592-3.

A644. Writing Objectives for Bibliographic Instruction in Academic Libraries: a summary of the proceedings of Sessions of the Midwest Federation of Library Associations, Detroit, October 1-2, 1975. Kenosha, Wis.: Director's Office, Library Learning Center, University of Wisconsin-Parkside, 1976.

A645. Wyandt, Shristine R. A Librarian's Hints for Students. Hicksville, New York: Exposition, 1979.

A646. Wygant, A. C. "User Education." Texas Library Journal 59(Spring 1983): 15-7.

A647. Yaple, Henry M., comp. "Programmed Instruction in Librarianship: a classified bibliography of programmed texts and other materials 1960-1974." University of Illinois Graduate School of Library Science Occasional Papers (1976) no. 124.

School Libraries

S001. Althoff, R. H. "Instructional Development in the Elementary Learning Center." Media Spectrum 9 no. 1 (1982): 13.

S002. Arizzi, M. D. "Fun & Games With Dewey." Indiana Media Journal 2 (Spring 1980): 15-7.

S003. Ashley, R. "Tool for Library Evaluation; the national library skills test." Media Spectrum 9 (1982): 15.

S004. Baitinger, L. E. "Trying On New Media Skills: to Middleton K-12 students they feel like old shoes." Wisconsin Library Bulletin 73 (July 1977): 151-2.

S005. Baker, D. Philip. The Library Media Program and the School. Littleton, Colorado: Libraries Unlimited, 1984.

S006. Bard, Therese Bissen. School Libraries in Hawaii. ERIC Educational Document Reproduction Service, 1983. (ERIC Document Reproduction Service No. ED 239619).

S007. Beam, Karen G. "Library Instruction: teaching a survival skill." Hoosier School Libraries 14 (April 1975): 18-9.

S008. Beaton, K. J. "Teaching Information-Use." Library Association Record 77 (May 1975): 124.

S009. Beck, M. J. and Kuester, D. L. "Games for Goals." Media Spectrum 3 no. 1 (1976): 10-1.

S010. Beck, Margaret V. and Carney, Vera M. A Guidebook for Introducing Library Skills to Kindergarten and Primary Grades. Minneapolis: Denison, 1981.

S011. Beck, Margaret V. and Carney, Vera M. Guidebook for Teaching Library Skills. (Book 1, Using the Card Catalog. Book 2, Using the Dewey Decimal System. Book 3, Using Reference Materials.) Minneapolis: Denison, 1981.

S012. Behm, M. W. "How to Find Everlasting Peace and Happiness Via Library Skills Instruction." Ohio Association of School Librarians Bulletin 28 (October 1976): 12-5.

S013. Bell, Irene Wood and Brown, R. B. Gaming In the Media Center Made Easy. Littleton, Colorado: Libraries Unlimited, 1982.

S014. Bell, Irene Wood and Wieckert, Jeanne E. Basic Media Skills Through Games. Littleton, Colorado: Libraries Unlimited, 1979.

S015. Bell, Irene Wood and Wieckert, Jeanne E. Related Media Skills Through Games. Littleton, Colorado: Libraries Unlimited, 1979.

S016. Berg, Janne. "Encouraging Choice." Australian Journal of Reading 7 (November 1984): 205-9.

S017. Bertrand, L. and Klatt, J. "Mutant Melvil Ameliorates Media Skills." Wisconsin Library Bulletin 75 (March 1979): 71-3.

S018. "Bibliographic Instruction: a guide." Education Libraries 7 (Fall 1982): 45-60.

S019. Biddle, Michaelle L. "Planning and Design of the High School Library-Use Instruction Program." Catholic Library World 53 (November 1981): 160-3.

S020. Bienvenu, Martha and Others. comps. A Handbook for Student Librarians. Bulletin 1632. Baton Rouge, Louisiana: Louisiana State Department of Education, 1981. (ERIC Document Reproduction Service No. ED 213425).

S021. Biggs, M. M. "Forward To Basics in Library Instruction." School Library Journal 25 (May 1979): 44.

S022. Biggs, M. M. "Proposal for Course-related Library Instruction." School Library Journal 26 (1980): 34-7.

S023. "BL Backs School Project: the need to know." Library Association Record 80 (March 1978): 3.

S024. Blackwell, E. N. and others. "Sequence of Library Skills." Hoosier School Libraries 14 (Fall 1975): 18-21.

S025. Brenton, M. "Elementary School Library Media Curriculum." Bookmark 30 (Winter 1900). 314-24.

S026. Browning, E. K. "Solve the Mystery of Reference: use 'calendar clue'." School Library Journal 22 (October 1975): 71-4.

S027. Brumback, E. L. "School Media Program: the alpha and omega of life-long bibliographic skills." North Carolina Libraries 38 (Fall 1980): 14-6.

S028. Brun, L. "User Education [the junior and senior research paper]." Texas Library Journal 61 (Fall 1985): 72.

S029. Buchholz, K. "Teaching Research and Reference Skills in the Junior High." Ohio Media Spectrum 35 (Fall 1983): 9-10.

S030. Buckingham, Betty Jo. Comp. Library Media Skills Sampler. Volume I: a sharing of ideas from practicing school library media specialists in Iowa. Des Moines, Iowa: Iowa State Department of Public Instruction, 1984. (ERIC Document Reproduction Service No. ED 247927).

S031. Buddy, J. "If Only I Had Known." Ohio Media Spectrum 33 (July 1981): 8-11.

S032. Butz, M. N. "Teaching Library Skills Can Be Enjoyable." Hoosier School Libraries 17 (December 1977): 26-7.

S033. "Card Games in Library Instruction." Nebraska Library Association Quarterly 9 (Summer 1978): 16-7.

S034. Carhart, M. "Let's Go to the Library." Early Years 8 (November 1977): 37.

S035. Carpenter, M. "Task Card Instruction." Ohio Media Spectrum 30 (January 1978): 52-4.

S036. Carroll, F. L. Recent Advances In School Librarianship. New York: Pergamon Press, 1981.

S037. Charles, D. Calico Cat Meets Bookworm. Chicago: Children's, 1978.

S038. Chedsey, K. A. "All About the Library." Instructor 87 (November 1977): 124-125.

S039. Chernik, S. "Programed Library Skills Workbook: Tremper High School plan allows flexibility." Wisconsin Library Bulletin 74 (March 1978): 94.

S040. Childs, J. W. "Instructional Development — Where Are We?" Media Spectrum 9 (1982): 4.

S041. Chirgwin, John F. and Oldfield, Phyllis. The Library Assistant's Manual. 2nd rev. ed. London, Eng.: Clive Bingley, 1983.

S042. Christine, E. R. "Multimedia Library Skills for Today's Child: a suggested sequence." California Media and Library Educators Association Journal 1 (Winter 1978): 22-7.

S043. Chu, S. C., and Shellhase, J. "Special Health Sciences Library Skills For High School Students." Show-Me Libraries 34 (February 1983): 12-5.

S044. Clark, M. W. "Toot-Toot For Reading." Instructor 87 (November 1977): 47.

S045. Claver, P. "Librarians as Motivators." Catholic Library World 52 (July 1980): 13-6.

S046. Cleary, Florence D. Discovering Books and Libraries: a handbook for students in the middle and upper grades. 2nd ed. New York: Wilson, 1977.

S047. Colsher, J. and Follo, E. "Elementary Library Skills: a program which has been successfully implemented in the Grosse Pointe Public School system." Media Spectrum 9 no. 1 (1982): 9-10.

S048. Concannon, T. "Reading Games & Skill-Building Activities." School Library Journal 30 (May 1984): 40.

S049. Condit, M. O. "If Only the Teacher Had Stayed With the Class." Elementary English 52 (May 1975): 664-6.

S050. Conor, R. "New Slant On YA Service." Focus 31 (May 1977): 6.

S051. Corcoran, Eileen L. Gaining Skills in Using the Library: a workstudy book to improve library skills. Phoenix, Az.: Frank E. Richards, 1980.

S052. Corser, G. A. "Instructional Development: the

engineering of instruction." Media Spectrum 9 (1982): 5-6.

S053. Corser, M. S. "Media Specialist and Instructional Development." Media Spectrum 9 (1982): 3.

S054. Craig, R. "Information Skills and Curriculum Development." Library Review 31 (Autumn 1982): 187-8.

S055. Craver, Kathleen W. "Play Cats Eclectic!" School Library Journal 29 (April 1983): 34.

S056. Craver, Kathleen W. "Teaching Online Bibliographic Searching to High School Students." Top of the News 41 (Winter 1985): 131-8.

S057. Crowe, W. J. "Library Skills for Students: keeping pace." Ohio Library Association Bulletin 55 (April 1985): 22-3.

S058. Crump, Diana. "Card Catalog Bingo." Hoosier School Libraries 14 (Fall 1975): 21+.

S059. Crump, Diana. "Games for Teaching Library Skills." Indiana Media Journal 2 (Fall 1979): 19-21.

S060. Curriculum Guide for the Teaching of Media Skills, K-12. Oklahoma City: Oklahoma State Department of Education, Oklahoma Curriculum Improvement Commission, 1975. (Eric Document Reproduction Service No. ED 125655).

S061. Dequin, H. C. and Smith, J. "Learning Disabled Students Can Be Tutors in Library Media Skills." Top of the News 36 (Summer 1980): 352-6.

S062. Dermon, E. S. "Getting to Know the Library." Media & Methods 13 (April 1977): 54.

S063. DeSomogyi, A. "Make Your Point: library skills: now or never." School Library Journal 22 (November 1975): 37.

S064. Doyle, C. "Media for Library Skills Instruction." Previews 7 (February 1979): 2-8.

S065. Doyle, C. and Wehmeyer, L. W. Comps. "Library Media Center Skills." Booklist 71 (June 1975): 1001-3.

S066. Duryee, J. E. and Stoutjesdyk, D. "Developing a K-6

Media Center Skills Curriculum." <u>Media Spectrum</u> 6 no. 4 (1979): 19.

S067. Eisenberg, Michael. "Curriculum Mapping and Implementation of an Elementary School Library Media Skills Curriculum." <u>School Library Media Quarterly</u> 12 (Fall 1984): 411-8.

S068. Elliott, Anna Bunker. "Show Them with Pictures." <u>Momentum</u> 10 (February 1979): 17.

S069. Elza, B. and Maslar, I. "REFECOL: original project devised to encourage students to get to know a variety of reference materials." <u>Science Teacher</u> 42 (November 1975): 31-2.

S070. Eshpeter, B. "Whither the Goose That Laid the Golden Age?" <u>School Libraries in Canada</u> 1 (Spring 1981): 3-6.

S071. Fabian, W. M. and courtney, M. S. "Apple for the Librarian: microcomputer and instruction." <u>Show-Me Libraries</u> 33 (March 1982): 5-8.

S072. Farina, S. L. "Student Authors in the Library Learning Center." <u>Ohio Media Spectrum</u> 31 (Spring 1979): 34-7.

S073. Fast, E. T. "Why Susie Can't Use the Library." <u>Wilson Library Bulletin</u> 51 (May 1977): 732-3.

S074. Fiebert, E. E. "The Integration of Online Bibliographic Instruction Into the High School Library Curriculum." <u>School Library Media Quarterly</u> 13 (Spring 1985): 96-9.

S075. Foth, C. "Middle School Instruction At All Levels." <u>Nebraska Library Association Quarterly</u> 9 (Winter 1978): 16.

S076. Fredericka, T. M. "Senior Send-Off." <u>Ohio Association of School Librarians Bulletin</u> 28 (October 1976): 10.

S077. Garland, K. "Developing a Guide for the Teaching of Library Skills: a case study." <u>Ohio Association of School Librarians Bulletin</u> 28 (October 1976): 15-7.

S078. George, Mary W. and Hogan, Sharon A. "Information on Cards and What It All Means." <u>Research Strategies</u> 2 (Spring 1984): 88-97.

S079. Gibb, S. "Exhausting but Effective: teaching basic library skills." <u>California Media and Library Educators Association Journal</u> 2 (Winter 1979): 8-9.

S080. Gibson, Mary Jane and Kaczmarek, Mildred. <u>Finding Information in the Library: a guide to reference sources for Rochelle High School students.</u> 2nd ed. Illinois: Rochelle Township High School District 212, III, 1977. (ERIC Document Reproduction Service No. ED 161460).

S081. Gibson, Mary Jane and Kaczmarek, Mildred. <u>Student Activity Workbook for Use with Finding Information in the Library.</u> Rochelle, Illinois: Rochelle Township High School District, 1977.

S082. Gifford, Vernon and Gifford, Jean. <u>Effects of Teaching a Library Usage Unit to Seventh Graders.</u> Paper presented at the Annual Conference of the Mid-South Educational Research Association (13th, New Orleans, Louisiana, Novmeber 14-16, 1984). ERIC Document Reproduction Service, 1984. (ERIC Document Reproduction Service No. ED 254230).

S083. Glavich, M. K. "Boring and the Lively." <u>Learning Today</u> 12 (Summer-Fall 1979): 85-7.

S084. Good, B. L. "Please -- I Want To Do It Myself! Lakeview students learn skills in a planned program." <u>Wisconsin Library Bulletin</u> 73 (July 1977): 153-4.

S085. Gordon, C. "Teaching the Young to Use Indexes." <u>Indexer</u> 13 (April 1983): 181-2.

S086. Grant, L. T. "Library Lesson, Constructed On Piagetian Principles, For Use In Self-Service Elementary Instructional Media Centers." <u>Texas Library Journal</u> 53 (Winter 1977): 24-7.

S087. Grindeland, W. D. and Hildebrandt, L. L. "Project Publish." <u>Wisconsin Library Bulletin</u> 77 (Summer 1981): 70-1.

S088. Grooter, L. E. "Library Media Skills Guide From Wisconsin School Library Media Association." <u>Wisconsin Library Bulletin</u> 75 (March 1979): 66.

S089. Gustafson, Kent L. and Smith, Jane Bandy. <u>Research for School Media Specialists.</u> Georgia: University of Georgia. Department of Educational Media and Librarianship, 1982.

S090. Hale, Robert G. and Others. A Guide to School Library Media Programs. Hartford, Connecticut: Connecticut State Board of Education, 1982. (ERIC Document Reproduction Service No. ED 230201).

S091. Hamilton, L. "Suggestions for Secondary School Library Lessons." School Librarian 25 (September 1977): 217-20.

S092. Handbook for Elementary Library-Media Instruction. Rev. ed. Pleasant Hills, California: Contra Costa County Department of Education, Educational Media Services, 1975. (Eric Document Reproduction Service No. ED 125652).

S093. Hanson, M. "ID Applications for Basic Skills; teeming for middle schools." Media Spectrum 9 no. 1 (1982): 11-12.

S094. Hardison, D. A. and Moore, D. M. "Library Skills Via Videocassette: back to the drawing board." International Journal of Instructional Media 6 (1978-79): 101-5.

S095. Hart, Thomas L., ed. Instruction in School Media Center Use. Chicago: American Library Association, 1978.

S096. Haycock, C. A. "Information Skills in the Curriculum: developing a school-based continuum." Emergency Librarian 13 (September/October 1985): 11-17.

S097. Heather, P. "Research on Information Skills in Primary Schools." School Librarian 32 (September 1984):214-20.

S098. Hein, C. E. "Independent Study Guides: Mann Junior High students learn library media skills." Wisconsin Library Bulletin 73 (May 1977): 129-30.

S099. Hein, C. E. "Learning to Learn With Independent Study Guides." Peabody Journal of Education 55 (April 1978): 193-7.

S100. Hendley, Gaby G. Using the Microcomputer to Generate Materials for Bibliographic Instruction. ERIC Document Reproduction Service, 1984. (ERIC Document Reproduction Service No. ED 252190).

S101. Hendricks, B. P. "Student Survival Skills in a High

School Library." <u>South Carolina Librarian</u> 22 (Spring 1978): 12.

S102. Herring, James E. <u>Teaching Library Skills In Schools.</u> Berks.: NFER, 1978.

S103. Herring, James E. "User Education In Schools: purposes, problems, potentials." <u>School Librarian</u> 28 (December 1980):341-5.

S104. Herring, James E. "Where's 635?" <u>New Library World</u> 80 (January 1979): 7-9.

S105. Hinchliff, W. E. "RISE [Reform of Intermediate and Secondary Education] and Shine." <u>California Librarian</u> 36 (July 1975): 46-55.

S106. Hoagland, M. Authur. "Library Skills -- Caught or Taught." <u>Catholic Library World</u> 53 (November 1981): 173-5.

S107. Hodge, R. and Burgoon, C. "Library Skills-Learn and Apply." <u>Ohio Media Spectrum</u> 31 (Spring 1979): 48-9.

S108. Horton, J. S. "High School Graduate and the College Library." <u>Hoosier School Libraries</u> 17 (October 1977): 21-3.

S109. Houston, Shirley. "Atrisco Elementary, Albuquerque: our latest project is attempting to breathe some life into the Dewey Decimal System for fifth graders." <u>New Mexico Libraries Newsletter</u> 4 (February 1976): 3.

S110. Hughes, S. K. "K-12 Approach to Library Skills Instruction." <u>Colorado Libraries</u> 9 (June 1983): 12-7.

S111. Hyland, A. "Instructional Standards." <u>Ohio Association of School Librarians Bulletin</u> 28 (October 1976): 36-9.

S112. Hyland, A. "Profile of Library skills in Ohio." <u>Ohio Media spectrum</u> 31 no. 4 (1979): 12-7.

S113. "Individualized Instruction In elementary School." <u>South Carolina Librarian</u> 22 (Spring 1978):11.

S114. <u>Information Resources on Microcomputers in Library Instruction. A Selected ERIC Bibliography.</u> Syracuse, New York: ERIC Clearinghouse on Information Resources, Syracuse University, 1984. (ERIC Document Reproduction Service No. ED 254223).

S115. Irving, A. and Snape, W. H. Educating Library Users in Secondary Schools. (British Library Research and Development Reports; no. 5467). London, Eng.: British Library, 1979.

S116. Izumo, Patsy M. and Others. Hawaii School Library Media Centers: a manual for organization and services. Honolulu, Hawaii: Hawaii State Department of Education, Office of Library Services, 1976. (ERIC Document Reproduction Service No. ED 148375).

S117. Jay, H. L. Stimulating Student Search: library media/classroom teacher teachniques. Hamden, Conn.: Lib. Professional Publs., 1983.

S118. Johnston, M. K. Library Media Study Guides for Hatch High School Teachers. Texas: George Peabody College for Teachers, 1977.

S119. Jones, A. "User Education in Secondary School Libraries." School Librarian 30 (March 1982): 15–18.

S120. Jones, A. M. and Thieding, E. C. "Reference Skills On-Line: a computer assists individually planned instruction." Wisconsin Library Bulletin 72 (May 1976): 103–4.

S121. Karpisek, Marian E. Making Self-Teaching Kits for Library Skills. Chicago, Ill.: American Library Association, 1983.

S122. Keene, M. and Waity, G. A. "Media Center Uses Games for Individual Learning and For Fun." Wisconsin Library Bulletin (May 1976): 101–2.

S123. Keith, B. "Improved Media Skills, Services Goal of Library Training Program." Mississippi Libraries 43 (Spring 1979): 38–9.

S124. Kelly, Joanne and Others. Library Curriculum Guide and Handbook for Librarians. Rev. Ed. Illinois: Urbana School District 116, 1979. (ERIC Document Reproduction Service No. ED 213415).

S125. King, A. I. "Curriculum Guide for the Library Media Center." Unabashed Librarian 26 (1978): 22–5.

S126. Knepel, N. P. "Mix Skills With Fun in a Juvenile Correctional Institution Library." Wisconsin Library Bulletin 75 (March 1979): 57–8.

S127. Kouns, B. "Thirteen Steps to Library Orientation." School Library Journal 23 (March 1977): 125.

S128. Kuhlthau, Carol Collier. A Process Approach to Library Skills Instruction. Paper presented at the Annual Meeting of the American Association of School Librarians (Atlanta, Georgia, October 31 - November 4, 1984). ERIC Document Reproduction Service, 1984. (ERIC Document Reproduction Service No. ED 254233).

S129. Kuhlthau, Carol Collier. "A Process Approach to Library Skills Instruction." School Library Media Quarterly 13 (Winter 1985): 35-40.

S130. Kuhlthau, Carol Collier. School Librarian's Grade-by-Grade Activities Program: a complete sequential skills plan for Grades K-8. West Nyack, New York: The Center for Applied Research in Education, 1981.

S131. Lander, F. "Aides Acquire Marketable Skills." School library Journal 29 (August 1983): 34.

S132. Lander, F. "Handy Dandy AV Instructional Card." Ohio Media Spectrum 33 (March 1981): 15-16.

S133. Lankford, Mary D. Library Skills Handbook. (Book 1, Grades K-5, Book 2, Grades 6-8.) Irving, Texas: Irving Independent School District, 1979-1980.

S134. Lansner, H. "Special Report: making the very best of a bad thing." Wilson Library Bulletin 53 (February 1979): 456-7.

S135. Lashbrook, J. E. "Library Media Skills in the Classroom and the Library Media Center." Ohio Media Spectrum 37 (Spring 1985): 32-4.

S136. "A Library Media Guide for Vermont Schools. Montpelier, Vermont: Vermont State Department of Education, Division of Federal Assistance, 1981. (ERIC Document Reproduction Service No. ED 242341).

S137. Library Skills Curriculum Activities/Objectives, K-12. Old Town, Maine: Maine Educational Media Association, 1984. (ERIC Document Reproduction Service No. ED 252222).

S138. Lubans, John. "In Pursuit of the Educated Library User: a dilemma." Ohio Association of School Librarians and Educational Media Council of Ohio Bulletin (Joint Issue) 28 (October 1976): 7-9.

S139. Luskay, Jack R. "Current Trends in School Library
Media Centers." Library Trends 31 (Winter 1983): 429-
46.

S140. Mallett, Jerry J. Library Skills Activities Kit:
puzzles, games, bulletin boards and other interest-
rousers for the elementary school library. West
Nyack, NY.: Center for Applied Research In Education,
1981.

S141. Mallett, Jerry J. Library Skills Activity Puzzles
Services. (5 books. incl. Book Bafflers, Dictionary
Puzzlers, Lively Locators, Reading Incentives, and
Resource Rousers.) West Nyack, NY.: Applied Research
in Education, 1982.

S142. Malley, Ian. ed. Current R & D Projects in User
Education in the U.K. Background papers and presented
papers of a conference held at Loughborough University
of Technology on 22nd March 1979. Leicestershire,
England: British Library Information Officer for User
Education. Library. Loughborough University of
Technology, 1979.

S143. Mancall, Jacqueline C. "Training Students to Search
Online: rationale, process, and implication." Drexel
Library Quarterly 20 (Winter 1984): 64-84.

S144. Marantz, S. S. "Contemporary 398.2." Ohio Media
Spectrum 35 (Fall 1983): 15-7.

S145. Margrabe, Mary. "Library Media Specialist and Total
Curriculum Involvement." Catholic Library World 49
(February 1978): 283-7.

S146. Margrabe, Mary. The 'Now' Library Media Center: a
stations approach with teaching kit. Washington,
D. C.: Acropolis, 1977.

S147. Marks, J. S. "Learning Resources Center Orientation."
Texas Library Journal (Fall 1978): 199.

S148. Marland M. ed. Information Skills in the Secondary
Curriculum. New York: Methuen, 1981.

S149. Marshall, Karen K. Back to Books: two hundred library
games to encourage reading. Jefferson, NC.:
McFarland, 1983.

S150. Mary, Columba Offerman. "Let's Make Better Use of Our
Libraries." Clearing House 52 (October 1978): 61-64.

S151. McCarthy, P.B. "In-Service at Eisenhower IMC: helping students help themselves." Catholic Library World 49 (February 1978): 275-9.

S152. McDavid, B. "Blueprint for Reform." California Media and Library Educator Association Journal 7 (Fall 1983): 16-8.

S153. Mealy, Virginia. Library Skills: activities and games. Minnesota: Denison, 1981.

S154. Merriam, Joyce. Helping Students Make the Transition from High School to Academic Library: a report on a study of selected library instruction programs in Massachusetts. ERIC Educational Document Reproduction Service, 1979. (ERIC Document Reproduction Service No. ED 176783).

S155. Merrill, R. L. "Operation Cooperation, Mishawaka Style." Hoosier School Libraries 17 (October 1977): 25-6.

S156. Meyers, E. M. "Teaching Library Skills to Deaf Children." Catholic Library World 51 (September 1979): 58-60.

S157. Micetich, B. J. "Teaching Library and Research Skills: librarian, do I ever need your help!" Catholic Library World 56 (November 1984):187-90..

S158. Miller, G. "Orientation by Competency." School Library Journal 29 (March 1983): 128.

S159. Miller, J. M. "Information Caper." Mississipi Libraries 45 (Summer 1981): 43-4

S160. Miller, L. "Planning Media Skills Instruction to Correlate With Classroom Instruction." School Media Quarterly 8 (Winter 1980): 120.

S161. Miller, N.L. "Remote Control Tour; or, How to Escape the Beginning-of-school Library Orientation." Hoosier School Libraries 15 (December 1975): 43.

S162. Miller, Robert E. "Teaching Skills in the Retrieval and Utilization of Materials and Equipment for Students and Faculty." Catholic Library World 50 (March 1979): 327-9.

S163. Miller, Rosalind. "Why I Can't Create a Learning

Center: a description of a learning center program for the school media center." School Media Quarterly 3 (Spring 1975): 215-8.

S164. Morante, Rosemary and Others. Instruction in Library Media Skills. Supplement to a Guide to School Library Media Programs. Hartford, Connecticut: Connecticut Educational Media Association, 1984. (ERIC Document Reproduction Service No. ED 252210).

S165. Moskowitz, Michael Ann. "Developing a Microcomputer Program to Evaluate Library Instruction." School Library Media Quarterly 10 (Summer 1982): 351-6.

S166. Moskowitz, Michael Ann. "High School Libraries: how to introduce thirty sophomore classes to their high school libraries and have them come back again for more." Clearing House 54 (May 1981): 18-22.

S167. Moss, D. "Meeow...a Whatalogue?" Library Association Record 86 (February 1984): 73.

S168. Murratti, E. Reader's What? A Learning Package on the Reader's Guide to Periodical Literature. New Britain, Conn.: Murratti, 1978.

S169. Murroni, B. "Microcomputers & the School Library Media Program." Florida Media Quarterly 9 (Fall 1983): 20-1.

S170. "Nevada High Schoolers Get University Orientation." Library Journal 102 (August 1977): 1552.

S171. "No More Hush-Hush at this Library: airport 30 reading game teaches library skills." Unabashed Librarian 35 (1980): 28.

S172. Nordling, Jo Ann. Dear Faculty: a discovery method guidebook to the high school library. Westwood, Mass.: Faxon, 1976.

S173. Offerman, M. C. "Let's Make Better Use of Our Libraries." Clearing House 52 (October 1978): 61-4.

S174. Ogunsheye, F. Adetowun. A Perspective from Developing Countries. Background Paper No. 3. ERIC Educational Document Reproduction Service, 1982. (ERIC Document Reproduction Service No. ED 239615).

S175. Olaosun, A. "Teacher Education and School Libraries."

International Library Review 10 (October 1978). 389-96.

S176. Oldfield, Phyllis. "Initial Teacher Training in Library Usage: a survey." School Librarian 28 (June 1980): 120-4.

S177. Fallick, R. "Learning-to-Learn Skills -- an alternative to traditional library skills." Arkansas Libraries 42 (June 1985): 12-4.

S178. Pearson, L. "High School Library and the College-Bound Student." South Carolina Librarian 24 (Fall 1980): 11-3.

S179. Pender, K. "User Orientation in the Secondary School Library Resource Centre." School librarian 30 (June 1982): 100-6.

S180. Penn, P. "Children Learn Library Use; Marathon County public library has a K-8 plan." Wisconsin Library Bulletin 75 (March 1979): 55-6.

S181. "Pennsylvania Guidelines for School Library Media Programs." Harrisburg, Pennsylvania: Pennsylvania State Library, 1983. (ERIC Document Reproduction Service No. ED 241028).

S182. Peterson, D. "Commitment to Skills Basis of Junior High Plan." Nebraska Library Association Quarterly 9 (Winter 1978): 17-8.

S183. Petrone, C. G. "Produce Your Own Slide-Tapes." School Library Media Quarterly 9 (Spring 1981): 206-9.

S184. Pettigrew, William G. "New Space for Crowded School Library." American School and University 52 (May 1980): 135.

S185. Pila, M. "Mistaken Panacea." Learning Today 8 (Winter 1975): 58-9.

S186. Probasco, C. A. "Magic Circle...hub of learning." Nebraska Library Association Quarterly 9 (Winter 1978): 10-2.

S187. "Prototype Grade-by-grade Media Skills Continuum." Raleigh, Carolina: North Carolina State Department of Public Instruction, Division of School Media Programs., 1982. (ERIC Document Reproduction Service No. ED 233698).

S188. Puentes, M.   "California School Library Media
      Services: a position paper of the California Media and
      Library Educators Association." California Media and
      Library Educators Association Journal 2 (Winter 1979):
      3-4.

S189. Reid, D. "Patriotism for Infants." New Library World
      82 (May 1981): 81-2.

S190. Richards, F. "Publish, Produce and/or Perish." Media
      Spectrum 5 no. 4 (1978): 18+.

S191. Robbins, Wendy H. "Library Instruction: a partnership
      between teacher and librarian." Catholic Library
      World 55 (April 1984): 384-7.

S192. Rockwell, A. F. I Like the Library. New York: Dutton,
      1977.

S193. Ross, J. E. "Micro Software for Library Skills
      Instruction." School Library Journal 31 (November
      1984): 68-73.

S194. Sampson, M. "Literature Appreciation Learned Along
      With Library Skills." Nebraska Library Association
      Quarterly 9 (Winter 1978): 20-1.

S195. Sandys, M. "Happiness in Operation Discovery."
      California School Libraries 41 (May 1970): 150-1.

S196. Sawin, M. "High School Program Aimed Toward Lifelong
      Skills." Nebraska Library Association Quarterly 9
      (Winter 1978): 18-20.

S197. Scarpellino, A. "Two Children's Library Games."
      Unabashed Librarian 26 (1978): 27-8.

S198. Schon, Isabel and Hopkins, Kenneth D. Students'
      Attitudes and Use of the School Library (Eighth
      Grade). Procedures. ERIC Educational Document
      Reproduction Service, 1983. (ERIC Document
      Reproduction Service No. ED 247956).

S199. Schon, Isabel and Others. "Effects of a Special
      School Library Program on Elementary Students'
      Library Use and Attitudes." School Library Media
      Quarterly 12 (Spring 1984): 227-31.

S200. Schon, Isabel and Others. "A Special Motivational
      Intervention Program and Junior High School Student's

Library Use and Attitudes." Journal of Experimental
Education 53 (Winter 1984-85): 97-101.

S201. Schul, D. "Library Skills: one way or another." Ohio
Media Spectrum 31 (Spring 1979): 43-6.

S202. Schuster, Marie. The Library-Centered Approach to
Learning. Palm Springs, CA.: ETC, 1977.

S203. Schwarz, Edith and Others. Instructional Program
for Library/Media Centers. Elkins Park, Pennsylvania:
Cheltenham Township School District,1975. (ERIC
Document Reproduction Service No. ED 114082).

S204. Schwartz, M. E. "Research Skills and Materials:
helping seventh graders survive the system." Ohio
Media Spectrum 31 (Spring 1979): 41-3.

S205. "Secondary Children Not Book Trained." Library
Association Record 81 (March 1979): 115.

S206. "A Sequence of Library Skills." Hoosier School
Libraries 14 (Fall 1975): 18-21.

S207. Sexton, Kathryn. "Reference Work as a Teaching Tool."
Top of the News 40 (Fall 1983): 73-6.

S208. Shapiro, L. L. Teaching Yourself in Libraries: a
guide to the high school media center and other
libraries. NY.: Wilson, 1978.

S209. Shelton, John L. "Cultivating the Library Habit:
Project Uplift." Wilson Library Bulletin 50
(September 1975): 59-62.

S210. Sitter, C. L. "Library and Information Skills in
Public Schools in Colorado." Colorado Libraries 9
(June 1983): 5-11.

S211. Slick, M. H. "School Library Media Center Instruction
for Vo-Tech Students." School library Media Quarterly
11 (Winter 1983): 154-5.

S212. Sliney, M. "A User Education Programme in a Post-
Primary School." The School Librarian 33 (June 1985):
115-20.

S213. "SLJ Special Section: computer technology and
libraries." School Library Journal 31 (November
1984): 35-73.

S214. Smith, B. G. "How Do I Join, Please? Initial Library Instruction In a Secondary School." School Librarian 24 (June 1976): 109-11.

S215. Smith, J. M. and Winkworth, F. V. Library User Education: a bibliography of teaching materials for schools and colleges of further education. England: British Library Research & Development Department, 1978.

S216. Snyder, D. "What College-Bound Students Need to Know About Libraries." Idaho Librarian 35 (April 1983): 33-4.

S217. Sorensen, R. J. "School Library Media Programs and Basic Skills." Indiana Media Journal 6 (Spring 1984): 3-5.

S218. Soutar, J. "Upward Bound." Sourdough 18 (July 1981): 14+.

S219. Sparks, J. "Praise the Lord and Pass the Information." Tennessee Libraries 34 (Summer 1982): 25-7.

S220. Spirt, Diana L. Library-Media Manual. New York: Wilson, 1979.

S221. Stagg, S. and Brew, S. "Finding the Book You Want: an algorithm." School Librarian 25 (September 1977): 221-2.

S222. "Study Skills Related to Library Use: a K-12 curriculum guide for teachers and librarians. Honolulu, Hawaii: Hawaii State Department of Education, 1978. (ERIC Document Reproduction Service No. ED 169906).

S223. Tassia, M. "It's not Just a Game." School Library Journal 25 (March 1979): 105-7.

S224. Tepe, A. "We're Goin' to the Library." Ohio Media Spectrum 30 (January 1978): 50-1.

S225. "They Go Together." Learning Today 13 (Spring 1980): 76-7.

S226. Thomas, Lucille C., and Kirk, Thomas. Annotated Bibliography on Library Instruction in Elementary, Middle, and Secondary Schools. Chicago: American Library Association, 1976.

S227. Thompson, M. "AV Look At Library Skills; Slide Tape Show on Library Methodology." Instructor 84 (January 1975): 110.

S228. Toifel, R. C. and Davis, W. D. "Investigating Library Study Skills of Children in the Public Schools." Journal of Academic Librarianship 9 (September 1983): 211-5.

S229. Townsend, J. "Library Potpouri." Ohio Media Spectrum 31 (Spring 1979): 49-51.

S230. Trask, Margaret and Others. South Pacific Region Pilot Project on School Library Development: training programmes for teachers. Paris France: United Nations Educational, Scientific and Cultural Organization, General Information Programme, 1984. (ERIC Document Reproduction Service No. ED 247938).

S231. Trigg, S. "Use of the Library." School Librarian 29 (December 1981): 302-6.

S232. Turk, B. "Tradition! Tradition! or, Using Media to Teach Media Center Skills." Ohio Media Spectrum 33 (July 1981): 12-16.

S233. Valley, Ruth R. "If Learning Is Fun, Can Success Be Far Behind?" Hoosier School Libraries 14 (April 1975): 34+.

S234. Vollano, N. "Using Book Jackets to Teach Library skills." School Library Journal 27 (October 1980): 123.

S235. Walker, H. Thomas, and Montgomery, Paula Kay. Teaching Library Media Skills: an instructional program for elementary and middle school students. Littleton, Colo.: Libraries Unlimited, 1977.

S236. Waltzer, Margaret A. Is Your School Graduating Library Illiterates? New Orleans, La.: Margaret Allen Waltzer, 1981.

S237. Waltzer, M. A. "Library Instruction In Secondary Schools." Catholic Library World 48 (April 1977): 402-3.

S238. Warren, R. and Link, J. "High School Library Skills Program That Works." Media Spectrum 5 no. 4 (1978): 17.

S239. Wehmeyer, Lillian Biermann. The School Librarian as Educator. Library Science Text Series. Littleton, Colorado: Libraries Unlimited, 1976.

S240. Wehmeyer, Lillian Biermann and Skapura, R. J. "Leaping From the Curriculum in a Single Bound." California Media and Library Educators Association Journal 2 (Fall 1978): 18-23.

S241. Welch, C. B. "User Education." Texas Library Journal 59 (Summer 1983): 63-4.

S242. Wellner, H. J. "Dewey Can Be Fun; Kenosha Schools Produced Skills Videotapes and Games." Wisconsin Library Bulletin 75 (March 1979): 67-9.

S243. White, B. "Spontaneous Interaction in Library Media Center Programming: the teachable and the reachable moment." Arkansas Libraries 37 (September 1980): 24-5.

S244. White, C. and Coles, M. "Libraries and Laboratories." School Librarian 28 (September 1980): 237-42.

S245. Wieckert, Jeanne E. and Bell, Irene Wood. Media/Classroom Skills: games for the middle school. Colorado: Libraries Unlimited, 1981.

S246. Wight, Lillian and Grossman, A. Maximum Utilization of School Library Resources. Alberta, Canada: Edmonton Public Schools, 1977. (ERIC Document Reproduction Service No. ED 154781).

S247. Wilhelm, L. "Teaching Library Skills With Video Games." Wyoming Library Roundup 38 (Fall 1982): 22-3.

S248. Williams, D. T. M. "Media Skills by Level: the Michigan approach." Wisconsin Library Bulletin 73 (July 1977): 155-6.

S249. Williams, R. "Vermilion Middle School Attacks Decline of Library Skills." Ohio Media Spectrum 31 (Spring 1979): 38-40.

S250. Wilmer, K. G. "Mystery At the Library." School Library Journal 28 (May 1982): 24-6.

S251. Winkworth, F. V. User Education in Schools: a survey of the literature on education for library and information use in schools. London: British Library, 1977.

S252. Winter, Edith M. The Spice Series Duplicating Masters: library studies. (Vol. 1, Grades 3-6; Vol. 2, Grades 7-9.) Stevensville, Mich.: Educational Service, 1976.

S253. Wisconsin Library Association, Wisconsin School Library Media Association. Wisconsin Library Media Skills Guide. WI.: Wisconsin Library Association, 1979.

Public Libraries

P001. Beilke, Patricia F. "Library Instruction in Public Libraries: a dream deferred, a goal to actualize." Reference Librarian 10 (Spr-Sum, 1984): 123-133.

P002. Campbell, D. "User Education." Texas Library Journal 59 (Fall 1983): 87-8.

P003. Carpone, Jerry. "Library Use Instruction in the Small and Medium Public Library: a review of the Literature." Reference Librarian 10 (Spr-Sum, 1984): 149-157.

P004. Dietrich, Jerrolyn M. "Library Use Instruction for Older Adults." Candian Library Journal 41 (Aug., 1984): 203-208.

P005. Frey, A. L. and Spigel, S. "Practical Librarian: educating adult users in the public library." Library Journal (April 15, 1979): 894-6.

P006. Hendley, M. "Librarian As Teacher: research skills for library patrons at Kitchener public library." Ontario Library Review 63 (March 1979): 45-8.

P007. Hendley, M. "User Education: the adult patron in the public library." RQ 24 (Winter 1984): 191-4.

P008. Holloway, Carol. "Teaching the Research Paper at the Public Library." Community College Review 11 (Sum. 1983): 27-31.

P009. Lubans, John, comp. and ed. Educating the Public Library User. Chicago, Ill.: American Library Association, 1983.

P010. Olszewski, L. "Taming the Library Monster; a new twist to an old game promotes a public library as an inviting place." American Libraries 16 (February 1985): 114.

P011. Reilly, Jane A. "Library Instruction Through the

Reference Query." Reference Librarian 10 (Spr-Sum, 1984):135-148.

P012. Shelton, John L. "Cultivating the Library Habit." Wilson Library Bulletin 50 (Sep. 1975): 59-62.

P013. Shinn, Duane. How to Discover Gold in the Library: the library book: how to extract a wealth of information from your public library. Medford, Or.: Duann Shinn, 1977.

P014. Van Hoven, J. "Handicapped Adults In the Library." New Jersey Libraries 12 (April 1979): 14-5.

P015. Van Hoven, J. "Pioneering New Jersey Program Aids Troubled Patrons." Library Journal 104 (April 1, 1979): 789-90.

P016. Van Hoven, J. "Suggested Films for Use With Handicapped Adults." Film Library Quarterly 13 no.1 (1980): 27-30.

P017. Warncke, Ruth. Planning Library Workshops and Institutes. (Public Library Reporter Series: no. 17). Chicago: American Library Association, 1976.

P018. White, D. J. "Orientation Course Aids Staff On The Job." Canada Library Journal 36 (February-April 1979): 17-20.

P019. Wyandt, Shristine R. A Librarian's Hints for Students. Hicksville, New York: Exposition, 1979.

Author Index

Title Keyword Index

A276; A308; A362;
A373; A467; A606; A637
Computer assisted
instruction   A264;
S119
Computers   G018; G051;
A387; A388; A515;
A537; A570; S071;
S100; S114; S165;
S169; S193; S213
Correctional institutions,
juvenile   S126
Curriculum   G127; A169;
A407; A590; S025;
S060; S066; S067;
S096; S124; S125;
S137; S145; S148;
S222; S240

- D -

Departmental training   G030
Data base management   G141
Data base searching
see Online literature
retrieval
Deaf   A306; A526; S156
Developing countries   S174
Dewey Decimal   S002; S011;
S109; S242
DIHE   G044
Directory - Indiana   A534
Directory - Kansas   A476
Directory - Louisiana   A118
Directory - New England
A553
Directory - Virginia   A475
Directory - Wisconsin
G074; G131
Disabled persons
see Handicaps
Dissertations   A012
Dorset Institute of Higher
Education   G044

- E -

Earlham College   A162
East Carolina University
A238

Education   A018; A079;
A184; A312; A468; A576
Elementary schools   S025;
S066; S086; S092;
S097; S113; S199
Engineering   A038; A180;
A193; A234; A342;
A343; A429; A561;
A579; A596; A600; A603
England   A378
English   A005; A196; A208;
A521
Environmental sciences
A424; A431
Evaluation   G020; G031;
G038; G047; G053;
G081; G089; G126;
G137; A008; A044;
A062; A078; A149;
A171; A180; A181;
A225; A250; A256;
A261; A263; A268;
A301; A316; A428;
A458; A461; A525;
A557; A618; S003

- F -

Faculty   A095; A158; A196;
A214; A236; A299;
A331; A374; A401;
A470; A483; A532;
A569; A632; S172
Films   A549; P016
Foreign students   A086;
A227; A344; A375; A421
Forestry   A431
Freshmen, college   A005;
A077; A208; A276;
A282; A497; A521; A611

- G -

Games   G013; G093; A347;
S013; S014; S015;
S033; S048; S059;
S122; S149; S171;
S197; S223; S245; S247
Geography   A030; A616; S153
Geology   A241

German Democratic Republic
  G122; A352; A360
Goals and objectives G098;
  A115; A167; A328;
  A410; A644; S219
Government documents G116;
  A125; A213; A528
Grade 5 S109
Grade 7 S082; S204
Grade 8 S198
Grades K-3 S010
Grades K-8 S011; S041;
  S047; S130; S149;
  S153; S180; S186
Grades 3-6 S252
Grades 5-8 S046
Graduates A153; A160;
  A228; A229; A283; A468
Grants A369; A619
Graphics G006; G015; G050;
  G064; G066; G077;
  G078; G084; G108;
  G109; G110; G117;
  G136; G139; A042; 045;
  A447
Grumman Aerospace
  Corporation A222
Guides and handbooks G004;
  G033

- H -

Handbooks
  see Guides and handbooks
Handicaps G003; S061;
  P014; P016
Harvard University A054;
  A303
Hawaii S006; S116
Health sciences A292;
  A562; S043
High schools S019; S028;
  S043; S051; S056;
  S074; S080; S081;
  S091; S100; S101;
  S115; S118; S120;
  S129; S142; S148;
  S166; S170; S172;
  S179; S191; S196;
  S205; S208; S212;
  S237; S238; S249; S252

Hiram College A574
History A211; A556
Humanities A604
Humor A385
Hunter College A028
Hunter Midtown Library
  A199

- I -

Illinois libraries A120
Indexes A559; S085
India A138; A489
Instructional materials
  G055; A393; A394
International users A327
Iowa S030

- J -

Japan A182
Junior high schools S029;
  S051; S091; S098;
  S115; S120; S142;
  S148; S179; S182;
  S191; S200; S205;
  S212; S237; S249
Junior colleges
  see Community colleges

- K -

Kits S140

- L -

Laboratories S244
Law A074; A075; A084;
  A093; A096; A117;
  A164; A289; A417;
  A418; A499; A510;
  A545; A602
Lawrence Library A619
Lawrence University A580
Learning disabled students
  A077
Leicester Polytechnic
  University A072
Libraries, academic A001-
  A648